D1329820

Eating Vegan
in Philly

Eating Vegan in Philly

Vegan City Guides

by
Vance Lehmkuhl

SULLIVAN
STREET
PRESS

Published by Sullivan Street Press, Inc., New York

Digital ISBN: 978-0-9976663-3-5
Print ISBN: 978-0-9976663-4-2

Contents

Introduction
Vegan City Guides

Vegan City Guides began as a conversation with food blogger, Paul Graham, after we published his book, *Eating Vegan in Vegas*. In 2012, we both agreed that there needed to be a way for vegans and vegan-friendly people across the county to learn about each other and what was happening in the various communities that supported a vibrant vegan food culture. As Paul put it, we needed to build bridges.

It became apparent as we traveled throughout the country that there was indeed a large and growing vegan food culture flourishing in many cities and towns that we normally don't associate with this attention to what we eat. Even in some of the most meat-oriented areas of the country, where the largest part of their economy derives from the raising and selling of beef cattle, there are signs in grocery stores alerting shoppers that they sell vegan foods.

The world has changed a great deal since that fateful discussion in 2012. The newest volume in **Vegan City Guides**, *Eating Vegan in Philly*, has shown us what is possible and from where this commitment to a plant-based diet has sprung. Philadelphia is where both the vegetarian and vegan movements began. For those who travel to Philadelphia for the history lessons, this new volume will be a source of great interest as to both the history of these two movements as well as the history of the restaurants that were actively involved in promoting a plant-based diet for all. Of course, what it also offers is the most comprehensive listing of vegan and vegan-friendly restaurants in and around Philadelphia.

As we continue to provide the vegan traveler—whether on the road for business or pleasure—with new volumes in the series, please join us at our Facebook page with comments about your travels and discoveries (facebook.com/eatingveganin). The building of bridges cannot continue without the active participation of everyone.

Foreword

It's no secret that Philadelphia is now an East Coast hot spot for vegan dining. *VegNews* recognized the city as such a couple years back in a head-to-head contest with Washington, DC. And the papers of record in both DC and New York City have done features making this point.

Here's another indicator: there was a time when there were so few truly vegan-friendly places in Philly that I had eaten at all of them. For a time, I was able to keep track of each new entry as it appeared. That time is happily long gone, as venues of all kinds increasingly see the value of appealing to those forgoing meat and dairy. And in my role as an occasional features writer and then vegan columnist for the *Philadelphia Daily News* over the past 15 years, I've contributed more than 200 articles covering this shift in thinking.

Some of those were collected in my previous book from Sullivan Street Press, *V for Veg: The Best of Philly's Vegan Food Column*. But this volume seeks to combine my take on the vegan scene with "news you can use"—a heapin' helpin' of places to find vegan food in Philadelphia, backed up by big-picture context.

Clearly this is largely for vegan travelers coming to (or considering coming to) Philadelphia, to get you up to speed immediately and help out in those situations where you find yourself with an unbooked meal and want to find something edible—and maybe incredible—nearby. But I'm hoping Philadelphia vegans will also enjoy and benefit from this book.

Philadelphia has become abundant enough in vegan offerings that this project doesn't comprise every single place in town that has a vegan option or two (sorry!), and certainly there will be even more growth in the future. The idea here was to choose a healthy sample of vegan-friendly joints (including, of course, all of Philly's vegan restaurants) and provide some idea of what they're coming up with to offer vegans, with an emphasis on those that have blazed local vegan trails, providing background perspective that may help readers choose what, where, and when they want to eat.

So there are chapters covering the history of vegan-friendly dining starting from colonial days to the present; a firsthand look at one of the city's emerging vegan traditions, the Best Vegan Cheesesteak in Philly Contest; and a couple bulleted lists for quick reference. I hope this will serve to lead all readers to the dish that persuades them that vegan-wise, Philly is the place to be.

Let me take this opportunity to thank Cynthia, Skyler, and Mariah for eating with me when I just had to check a certain place out and for lovingly providing alternate perspectives on vegan food and many other topics. Thanks also to my editor at the *Daily News*, Laurie Conrad, for her steady guidance and to Deborah Emin at Sullivan Street Press for suggesting I write this book. It was a good idea.

Philly's Central Role in Early US Vegetarianism and Veganism

Philadelphia is known and loved as a city of history and innovation, so it makes sense that it has a rich history of veganism and vegetarianism: in fact, it's where the US vegetarian movement was born in 1817, and the city has helped further that movement in several ways over the past couple centuries.

Even in the eighteenth century, there were individual vegetarians in Philadelphia. Benjamin Franklin spent several years as a vegetarian, and as if his many other forward-looking inventions and innovations weren't enough, he's likely also the first American to promote the eating of tofu.

How did that happen? Well, while Franklin was living in London before the Revolutionary War, he apparently encountered the bean curd concoction and was fascinated enough by it that he obtained some of the "Chinese caravances," or soybeans, and had them shipped to Philadelphia botanist John Bartram.

"My dear ever friend," Franklin wrote, explaining that he was sending "some Chinese Garavances, with Father Navaretta's account of the universal use of a cheese made of them, in China, which so excited my curiosity, that I caused enquiry to be made of Mr. Flint, who lived many years there, in what manner the cheese was made; and I send you his answer."

Franklin continued by remarking that he believed there were soybeans growing in the colonies, "but I know not whether they are the same with these [enclosed], which actually came from China, and are what the Tau-fu is made of. They are said to be of great increase."

According to *Early History of Soybeans and Soyfoods Worldwide* by William Shurtleff and Akiko Aoyagi (Soyinfo Center, 2014), Franklin's letter is the earliest-known historical document by an American or in connection with America that mentions tofu by name. Bartram either planted the soybeans himself or distributed them to local farmers to try their hand, but no record has been found showing whether any were finally turned into tofu.

However, soybeans are turned into tofu daily at City Tavern, an Old City institution that traffics in historical authenticity, and that's where I learned about the Franklin-tofu axis. Here's the relevant passage from my column "Tofu on the Colonial Table" (August 8, 2013):

City Tavern owner and executive chef Walter Staib said adding a tofu entrée was "one of the best decisions I ever made," as the dish has wound up "a top seller" at City Tavern.

The straight-off-the-menu version is vegetarian, but is breaded with egg and served on linguine that also has egg; the vegan alternative—which Staib noted "tastes just as good"—is a broiled tofu served on a bed of seasonal veggies.

Was it the letter that inspired the addition, or was that a convenient excuse to diversify the menu? Staib allowed that, "I was getting a lot of requests for vegetarian options," and having researched the Franklin tofu issue, he decided the time was right to do something tasty with the information.

So is this vegging up of historical menus stretching the notion of "authentic" to fit modern tastes and health concerns?

Not necessarily, Staib said. "In the 18th century, a lot of people were [plant-based eaters] not by choice, but by circumstance."

Addison concurred: In Colonial times, "there were a lot more vegetables and a lot more starches served" than present-day menus might indicate.

Even among those who had the means to feast on flesh, some intentionally cut back. Thomas Jefferson, a prodigious gardener, said he ate meat only "as a condiment to the vegetables which constitute my principal diet."

In the context of the times, he was a "near-vegan," said Staib.

Whatever the vegan leanings of Franklin, Jefferson, or other founding fathers, the founding men and women of the US vegetarian movement arrived in Philadelphia on June 15, 1817, in the form of a "Bible Christian" congregation that set up a church at 10 N. Front Street. The sect was an offshoot of the Swedenborgian New Jerusalem church (Swedenborg was understood by many eighteenth- and nineteenth-century followers to be a vegetarian, though there is no such evidence in the historical record). A key principle of the Bible Christians was abstention from alcoholic drinks and animal flesh, ideas that might generously be termed "unpopular" in the nineteenth century, and 41 congregants fled England and followed William Metcalfe to Philadelphia in search of religious tolerance.

From the congregation's earliest days, Metcalfe preached at the church and around town and brought in visiting speakers who would orate on the subject of the "all-vegetable diet," as it was sometimes called. The two most significant were Bronson Alcott and Sylvester Graham.

Alcott, the father of Louisa May Alcott (born on Germantown Avenue in Philadelphia during Alcott's brief career move to the Delaware Valley), never became a Bible Christian, but he took the sect's ethical principles seriously and even extended them somewhat a decade later with his cofounding of Fruitlands. This was an all-vegan utopian commune on farmland in Harvard, Massachusetts, where 14 people attempted to live without any animal products (including honey) and raise their own food without animal labor. They also eschewed cotton and other common products of slave labor, with a social justice grasp of veganism's larger message that today we call "intersectionality."

However, such pioneering ideals still had blind spots, and from Louisa May's account, it seems a big one was Alcott's tacit assumption that women, and especially Mrs. Alcott, would take up most of the slack for the missing work animals, while he and other men contributed to the more philosophical work that needed to be done—sitting and talking "utopia" for hours at a time. Combine this interpersonal hubris with unlucky weather and an ill-planned agricultural workflow, and the whole community wound up failing before the end of its first year. It stands as a historical example of vegan ideals prominently but very imperfectly implemented in early America, a planted seed that failed to flower.

Sylvester Graham's harvest was more bountiful. Not only did his popular whole-wheat "Graham bread" make his name a household word (as the later mainstreamed "Graham cracker"), but Graham's oratory was renowned nationally; his ideas were collected and promoted in a popular periodical, the *Graham Journal*; and "Grahamite" followers even established boardinghouses in Philly and other cities where like-minded individuals might stay, eat, and socialize according to Graham's principles of temperance and vegetarian foods.

Philadelphia, and Sylvester Graham himself, figured prominently in the creation of the American Vegetarian Society (AVS) in 1850 by Graham, Metcalfe, and William Alcott (Bronson's second cousin, another longtime veg-head). After a founding convention in New York City, the society's first official meeting took place in Philadelphia's Bible Christian Church on September 4, 1850. AVS promoted vegetarian precepts (then intertwined with pacifism, women's suffrage, and the fight for the abolition of slavery) across the nation via literature, guest tours, and events such as the New Jersey Vegetarian Festival of 1853.

The AVS flourished for a few years, but with the advent of the Civil War, abolition's fight took center stage and the group, with dwindling membership, broke up. Yet Philadelphia's Bible Christian Church continued to make history with its key role in the 1886 founding of a new national group, the Vegetarian Society of America, by Henry S. Clubb, creating a network of chapters across the nation (including, in 1890, the Philadelphia Vegetarian Society) that lasted up to Clubb's death in 1921.

The Pre–"Vegan Scene" Days

Philadelphia lays claim to a lot of firsts, but America's first big-city vegetarian restaurant is not one of them. The aptly named Vegetarian Restaurant No. 1 opened in New York City in 1895, and as in other realms, Philly long played a sort of second fiddle to NYC's vegetarian and vegan dining scene.

It's not even clear when the first vegetarian restaurant opened in Philly, but a vegetarian restaurant called Physical Culture was running at 25 S. 9th Street by 1908. Others from this era include the Hygienic Cafe on Walnut Street and the Good Health Restaurant on Market Street across from the legendary Lit Brothers department store.

There were other vegan-friendly venues here and there throughout the early twentieth century, but they are largely shrouded in obscurity—not until the late 1970s did all-vegan operations start gaining traction and publicity. That's largely because in the 1970s, the counterculture of the previous decade went behind the counter to start businesses, and in Philadelphia as elsewhere, this led to a profusion of natural-foods stores and veggie-oriented restaurants. One that's still around is Essene, a large natural-foods market that opened on South Street in 1970 after a brief incarnation as a juice bar off Rittenhouse Square (it's now on 4th Street a couple blocks down from South).

Essene, along with other smaller health-food stores in the area, established an important outlet for organic produce and veggie-friendly foods at the epicenter of Philly's counterculture, acquainting meat-eating foodies with vegan options and providing an anchor for vegan-friendly startups. The store served as a community hub for forward-thinking eaters and hosted regular dinners where many vegetarians and vegans over the years met and networked.

There were other veggie-oriented health-food stores here and there, some of which had a big influence on the city's later vegan growth. A nut store, Center Foods, started at Broad and Pine in 1980. It then evolved into a natural groceries market that moved to 16th and Locust in 1995. Christina Pirello, whose *Christina Cooks* TV show on PBS brought macro- and plant-based cooking to millions, got much of her start at Center as well as in Malaga, New Jersey, where she perfected her baking and desserts.

In 1981, a vegetarian grill opened in the Reading Terminal Market, one that would, over decades, evolve into a vegan grill and much more. Basic 4 Vegetarian Cafe (or, as its hanging sign said, Basic 4 Vegetarian Snack Bar) was, at its opening, the first African American tenant in the ninety-year-old market.

In a 2012 *Philadelphia Tribune* article ("Basic 4 Cafe Thrives for Decades at the Terminal," June 9, 2012), Basic 4 manager Lisa Tynes spoke about her mother, Alfoncie B. Austin, a dynamic Seventh-Day Adventist who created the entire menu and personally cooked the hot "meat" sandwiches to order but also had carrot tuna at the ready: "I just think that she's remarkable to have been a pioneer in this area. My mom is an excellent cook, so she could have done soul food. She could have gone in any direction, but she chose this and it's just amazing."

Basic 4 was a welcome oasis of tasty nonviolent foods within a space flooded with traditional, "authentic," animal-based foods. Austin sold a lot of regular-cheese sandwiches but added vegan cheeses in 1992 and eventually went that route. Also in the 1990s, she developed her own vegan mayonnaise that you could get on your "Phillysteak"—likely the first regular-menu vegan chees-esteak in Philadelphia.

In 2002, I wrote a *Philadelphia City Paper* cover story on the growth of vegan dishes in Chinatown restaurants throughout the 1990s, with much attention to Harmony (now New Harmony), which seemed to have spurred more vegan inclusiveness among many of its colleagues, some adding more inventive vegan options to traditional menus, others opening all-vegan restaurants. For that piece, I spoke to Jenny Tang about Harmony's origin story:

> "My grandparents had a restaurant called the Mayflower, where my father [George Tang] worked, and when it closed in 1989, he opened Harmony. The Mayflower was not a vegetarian restaurant, but they had some of this food," she said, referring to the modified temple cuisine that is Harmony's hallmark.
>
> Harmony's fare is not strictly temple cuisine, Jenny Tang says, but her father does have a Buddhist background and modified the dishes slightly for a Chinatown palate. Other alumni of the Mayflower, some of whom worked at Harmony early on, followed in George Tang's footsteps with their own variations.

Other parts of town also saw vegan-friendly growth during this pivotal time. An upscale vegan restaurant called Richard's, in Voorhees, New Jersey, became a trendy plant-based destination for some South Jerseyans and for Philadelphians in the know. Back in Philly, the Natural Foods Eatery opened right on Broad Street (at Locust), serving an all-vegan menu without categorizing it as such.

Soon the vegetarian restaurant Govinda's opened a few blocks farther south on Broad. In the next decade, the operation would morph to concentrate on a side grill called Govinda's Gourmet to Go—a fast-food diner that's all-vegan except for the mozzarella cheese on some sandwiches. With that running well, owner Howard Brown, known as Hari, converted and rebuilt the previous main restaurant space into the Bakhti Garden, opening it in October 2016.

While vegan restaurants slowly started appearing, mainstream restaurants began adding explicitly vegan items. Sometimes this was just one basic veggie burger, but other restaurant chains such as Adobe Cafe (in South Philly and Roxborough) and Gianna's Grille (off South Street and off Rittenhouse Square) essentially split their menus in two, replicating most if not all of the regular menu in vegan form.

Any place that catered to vegans—especially at a time when most people hadn't yet heard the word—deserved kudos. But vegans were incensed when it was discovered that Gianna's had (unwittingly?) begun using a veggie cheese that contained casein, a cow's-milk protein, and worse, the initial reveal was denied and covered up before management admitted the fault. Gianna's, which took over the location of the legendary Levis Hot Dogs (one of the first hot-dog joints in America), eventually closed in 2009, with the old Levis location reopening the next year as the all-vegan Blackbird Pizzeria.

The new century saw the rise of vegan enterprise in the prepared-foods sector as well. Fresh Tofu, Inc., had started up in Allentown in the mid-1980s. At the turn of the century, Gene He left his Chinese restaurant job to start a tofu company, Nature Soy. Moshe Malka created an eclectic (though vaguely Middle Eastern) line of vegan snacks, noodle bowls, and sandwiches, which he managed to place at a couple Philadelphia 7-Eleven locations. Then in 2010, he expanded to nearly all the 7-Elevens in the Delaware Valley, marking a huge win for the availability of vegan foods.

Meanwhile, up north, Rich Landau had been experimenting with vegetarian flavors and textures at a veggie juice-bar-turned-lunch-counter in the corner of Nature's Harvest health food store in Willow Grove, Pennsylvania, since the mid-1990s.

Without formal culinary training—his education consisted largely of hanging around kitchens and bars where he worked—he started investigating what turned out best in a meatless or dairy-free setting, and the food started intriguing more customers to try this Horizons Cafe, with its brashly self-conscious slogan, "Food of the Future."

Landau expanded the business laterally, growing from an instore stand into an adjunct one-room operation connected to the health-food store. Finally, in 2001, he moved a couple doors down into a larger standalone space decorated in a vibrant Tex-Mex style and featuring an open kitchen, a night-and-day contrast to the previous candlelit, cloth-cloaked iteration of the cafe.

It was at this location that his future partner, Kate Jacoby, started as a pastry chef's assistant and soon moved up in that job, while also moving into Landau's heart. They married in 2004 and catered their own wedding.

Now, in many ways, Landau was on the top of the heap: from a humble juice bar to a thriving suburban destination for Philadelphia foodies, he'd become the proverbial big fish in a small pond. But he needed more room to swim.

How Philly Became a Vegan Dining Mecca

Maybe it's my relentless, wide-eyed, Pollyannaish optimism about vegan foods' appeal. Or maybe—just maybe—it's a keen eye for big moments in the history of Philly veggie-dom. Either way, I think most would agree that my *Daily News* features section cover story "Cream of the Crop: They're Out to Open Philly's Best Veggie Restaurant" (February 2, 2006) pretty much nailed it in suggesting the move of Horizons Cafe from Willow Grove into Philadelphia proper would "shake up the Philly restaurant scene" while also overturning stereotypes and converting people to a plant-based diet.

Looking back on it, of course, it's a no-brainer, and realistically, it was obvious to anyone who was paying attention that this was going to be a historic moment for Philly. In that article, Landau noted that "Philadelphia's dining experience right now is at such a great new level, gets better year after year—and yet after all this time there's no signature vegetarian restaurant in Philadelphia."

Jacoby added, "Back when Rich opened Horizons Cafe he didn't want to advertise that it was a 'vegetarian' place because he figured so many people would be, you know, resistant—but on our business cards we're now printing 'New Vegan Cuisine' because we feel like the climate has changed so much."

The rest is vegan history: by the end of that year, Horizons off South Street had already established itself as a fresh, must-try restaurant and was providing food so provocative that it made many reconsider their food choices. In that same article, one completely nonvegetarian Horizons fan says, "Whenever I eat at Horizons I find myself asking . . . 'now, why is it I need to eat meat, again?'"

Soon, Horizons was showing up in *Philadelphia* magazine's ranking of the city's Top 50 Restaurants. National attention came first from *VegNews* magazine, which named it Restaurant of the Year, then from the James Beard Foundation, which booked Landau and Jacoby to showcase their cooking at the prestigious James Beard House in New York City, breaking with tradition to spotlight a vegan restaurant for the first time.

Meanwhile, though, Landau was passing on both his self-taught vegan cooking style and his decade and a half of food-service experience to a staff of young would-be chefs and would-be vegans. He made a big enough impression on them that at least four have gone on to establish what might be considered the pillar venues of Philly's vegan dining scene: Mark Mebus with Blackbird Pizza, Nicole Marquis with HipCityVeg, Rachel Klein with Miss Rachel's Pantry, and Ross Olchvary with New Hope's Sprig and Vine.

Mebus has expanded Blackbird's footprint to Brooklyn in a collaboration with Champs Diner called Screamers Pizza, and Marquis has opened—in addition to four HipCityVeg locations (three in Philly, one in DC)—two vegan bars, Bar Bombón (three doors down from the first HipCityVeg) and, next to a 13th-Street porn shop, Charlie Was a Sinner.

A 2012 *V for Veg* column rounded up these reflections from the four:

Rachel Klein: "'Make sure, even if it takes longer, to do it right,' is something [Rich Landau] would say. 'It might just be just another dish to you, but it's someone's dinner.' There aren't many places to work at and learn that kind of thing. You don't want to compromise and cook with meat just to [learn from a good chef]. I appreciate all he taught me."

Nicole Marquis: "Consistency is our top priority [at the then newly-launched HipCityVeg]. We want the customer to be able to depend on it. That was Rich's thing: You'd see him watching every single plate that went to the table to be sure it was the best it could be for the guest experience."

Mark Mebus: "Rich is the guy who taught me how to make food taste good. Working side by side with him is really where I came to make food the way I wanted it to taste, and that is a skill I can only credit to him. I like the idea of quick-service establishments because I feel like I can connect a little more with the customer base. I enjoy making high-end foods [and] I try to bring as much of that to the table here as I can."

Ross Olchvary: "From working my way up the ladder there, I learned a lot about how to run a kitchen, about flavor pairings. Especially in the early days at Horizons, the menu focused on ethnic cuisines—Latin and Caribbean dishes, Mediterranean dishes and definitely some Asian influence. Seeing ingredient pairings through the eyes of a trained chef definitely helped me build my base arsenal of flavors. When I started at Horizons, no one was even talking about using local ingredients. I think Rich just showed, and I learned, that there's lots of room to be more creative with vegetables—there's so much more you can do with 'em."

Those four were steeped in Horizons' ethos and methods. One cook, Fernando Peralta, didn't last long at Horizons. Both he and his former boss agree he was more focused on doing things his own way, developing his own place—still vegan but more casual and more health-focused. That notion soon developed into Vgë Café in Bryn Mawr, which became a Main Line mainstay and led to a franchise store opening in Atlanta. In late 2016, Peralta, following the path taken by Landau and Jacoby, moved his successful operation from the 'burbs into the heart of Philadelphia and relaunched as PlantPure Cafe, a pioneering fast-food joint adhering to the strict Caldwell Esselstyn / T. Colin Campbell view, eliminating, for instance, almost all added oils.

I should note that Vegan Treats in Bethlehem, which opened in 2000, spent a few years impressing the local residents but by this point had also established a presence—and a name—in Philadelphia, as multiple Philly outlets including Blackbird and Govinda's carried their vegan cupcakes and other pastries, which impressed vegans and mainstream eaters alike, helping dispel the notion that animal-free treats suffered by comparison to the original.

Meanwhile, Landau and Jacoby were enjoying the success and accolades of their serious vegan dining experience, but Landau felt the format they'd established was hemming in creativity to some extent and possibly blocking even greater success, as he explained in a *V for Veg* column:

> "As much as we felt that our big plates really were unique and stood up, we wanted to make everything more approachable. At Horizons, some people never tried our braciole or our hearts of palm cake because they would always order the grilled seitan or the Pacific Rim tofu."
>
> (Guilty as charged!)
>
> "I think a lot of people never wanted to make the commitment to try new things because it was an entrée size—like the last mushroom dish we had: It was a whole roasted maitake mushroom over a stew of fingerling potatoes and leek ash. It was one of my favorite entrées we've ever done, yet a lot of people didn't order it because it is a commitment on a plate. Now as a smaller portion, they're going to be able to mix and match and get a lot of different tastes of Vedge."

So in 2011, Horizons was closed and the team opened Vedge, the restaurant that's now become synonymous with great vegan dining in the Delaware Valley. What Horizons did for vegan eating in Philadelphia itself, Vedge now carried to a national stage by mixing the vegetable-centric "farm-to-table" approach with a commitment to upscale dining excellence and showcasing delightful new dishes with flavors that always surprised and yet seemed inevitable.

A particularly good example of the national acclaim that rolled in came from *GQ*'s Alan Richman, very much a nonvegan who trafficked in cartoonish stereotypes of barely "tolerable" vegan food and "humorless" vegans—until he dined at Vedge. He wound up including it in his top 12 restaurants of 2013 ("The Perfect Night Out: The 12 Most Outstanding Restaurants of 2013," February 18, 2013), calling it a "great" dining experience: "The food and service traveled to a dimension in the culinary world where veganism has never been and where vegetables in general rarely go." Richman continued, "I had no idea so much flavor could be delivered without butter, cream, milk, eggs, and other kitchen staples," adding that "every dish tasted better than I expected it would" and concluding that every dish "had extraordinary balance and savoriness. Nothing was absent from this meal."

Of course, while the influence of Landau and Jacoby was huge, it wasn't the only source of vegan expansion in Philadelphia. Widening the trail blazed by Horizons, Mark McKinney, who went vegan in the late 1990s, began designing vegan specialties at the bars for which he cooked, and soon after Vedge opened, several key watering holes became very vegan-friendly, quickly outpacing competitors who were sticking to the single veggie burger or meatless steak sandwich option.

Among these vegan-friendly venues were Cantina Dos Segundos, Cantina Los Caballeros, Royal Tavern, and Khyber Pass. This latter joint just off 2nd and Chestnut was an epic dive bar in the 1990s with one of the best live-music scenes in Old City Philly, so thoroughly street-level eclectic that they even allowed the likes of me to play there a couple times. But the place underwent a transformation from Eliza Doolittle into My Fair Lady: the cramped, smoky stage and tiny, crowded dance floor were replaced by a sedate dining room, and the beer-and-beef menu blossomed with creative down-home vegan options like BBQ pulled pork, fried chicken, catfish, Italian sausage, coleslaw, and buttered popcorn—all in 100 percent animal-free versions.

Khyber Pass's transformation included just one menu shift, but this change was emblematic of Philly bars recognizing the competitive value of real vegan options—not just one item to defuse the "vegan veto" but a wider palette for health-conscious and/or veg-curious drinkers tired of the same old bar food—and McKinney's bars (which shared the same owner) were among the leaders of this trend.

By the time Vedge was gaining national recognition, more vegan, near-vegan, and vegan-friendly spots were peppering the greater Center City area, with Vegan Tree opening at the home of a former Loving Hut restaurant on South Street, Soy Cafe serving Northern Liberties, P.S. & Co. joining the crowd around Rittenhouse Square, Sweet Freedom offering allergen-free baked goods on South Street (later expanding to Bryn Mawr and Collingswood, New Jersey), and Vegan Commissary, based in South Philly, opening a storefront to complement its catering and wholesale-foods endeavors.

The year 2014 saw a few more envelope-pushing developments, one out in Jenkintown and the other right across the street from Khyber Pass. In Jenkintown, a new vegan restaurant called Flora opened, noteworthy for being launched by a team of nonvegans who saw the opportunity in serving a vegan clientele. Meanwhile, down in Old City Philadelphia, the Irish bar The Plough & the Stars began to tap the skills of newly vegan chef Lenka Zivcovic for a series of alternate-Thursday vegan tasting dinners that helped launch Zivcovic—"Vegan Chef Lenka"—and her creative vegan dishes into prominence in the Philly vegan scene.

Landau and Jacoby made the case for great vegan food with not just brick-and-mortar outlets but cookbooks, with which home chefs could approximate some of the amazing dishes they'd enjoyed while eating out. After a hit-or-miss outing in 2004 with the *Horizons Cafe Cookbook* (Book Publishing Company), Landau and Jacoby stepped up their game for the 2008 *Horizons: New Vegan Cuisine* cookbook (Horizons; I contributed the preface, "Horizons Is a Peak Experience") and followed that with vegan instant classic *Vedge* (The Experiment, 2013). In fall of 2016, they launched the similarly impressive *V Street* cookbook (Harper Collins).

In all cases, the point was to call nonvegan diners' bluff in a helpful way: before the cookbooks, "people would often say, 'Wow, if I could cook this way, I'd be vegan!'" said Landau, adding, "but there's an implicit flip side here: 'Since I *can't* cook like this, I'm going to eat dead animal flesh.'" And "since we have to sleep at night, there was definitely a cause behind the cookbooks. We wanted to demystify vegan cuisine, to break down the barriers."

Other Philadelphia cookbooks making the vegan landscape a friendlier one came from authors such as Dynise Balcavage (*Urban Vegan*), gluten-free chef / food photog Allyson Kramer (*Great Gluten-Free Vegan Eats from around the World*), and Sweet Freedom's Allison Lubert (*Baking You Happy*). These and other authors bring an inspired creativity to making delicious vegan cooking more accessible, especially to those who wanted to try it out at home.

Making the food itself accessible are organizations such as the Philadelphia Orchard Project and commercial startups like Metropolis Farms, the first vegan-certified vertical farm in the United States. A company no one had heard of in January 2016, Metropolis had its lettuces and microgreens available in retail outlets like Essene Market by September of that same year. Metropolis joined established Philly vegan companies such as Michael's

Seitan and Brad's Kale Chips, whose offerings are found in stores and eateries across the Delaware Valley.

Vegan-prepared foods also flourish, with Rachel Klein of Miss Rachel's Pantry becoming renowned for her spreadable cheeses as well as a challah-based grilled cheese sandwich and with an increased reach for the low-key Vegan Commissary a few blocks away, which consistently provided a variety of vegan sauces and entrées to multiple Philly outlets. In 2016, the plant-based provider raised its profile with a line of lunch items at DiBruno Bros.—one of Philly's best-established bastions of old-school meat-and-cheese culture—and as the provider of vegan pepperoni and sausage to Slice Pizza, long a vegan-friendly haven with its optional Daiya. Upon opening its third location in Fishtown, Slice added vegan proteins to the existing veggie toppings available at all locations.

In late 2016, Landau and Jacoby took another step that may further solidify their dominant role in Philly's food scene—vegan and otherwise—with Wiz Kid, a simpler, more downscale concept with a signature vegan cheesesteak as its anchor. The wordplay in the name recalls both the Cheez Whiz featured on cheesesteaks (Wiz Kid's is rutabaga-based) and Landau's own persona as a self-taught "wizard" of food. Two locations (one a counter inside a new Center City Whole Foods, the other next door to V Street) opened in quick succession, quickly making Wiz Kid the second vegan fast-food chain in Philly, after HipCityVeg.

Thanks to years of hard work by Landau, Jacoby, and their protégés, plus a couple dozen other vegan pioneers, Philadelphia has become known as a "hot spot" for vegan cuisine, with both the *New York Times* and the *Washington Post* tipping readers to the news. Tourist agency Visit Philadelphia has spotlighted the trend in marketing literature, and as the trend continues and grows, it's safe to say that our town's horizons are bright.

Here's to the food of the future!

The Cheesesteak Contest and Other Big Food Events

Other than Ben Franklin and the whole founding-of-the-country thing, Philadelphia is known everywhere for two things: it's the city of Rocky, and it's the city of cheesesteaks.

While there are other pairings of cities with signature food items (Cincinnati/chili, Chicago/pizza, and New Orleans/gumbo), the strong tie between "Philly" and "cheesesteak" is reflected on countless menus in diners and sandwich shops across America, as though taking a sandwich you consider a cheesesteak and adding the word "Philly" to the name makes it tastier. These so-called Philly items encompass every imaginable variation/bastardization, and everyone visiting town knows they're supposed to grab the opportunity to have an "authentic" cheesesteak.

Of course, as in so many other areas, what constitutes "authentic" in terms of a cheesesteak is a disputed area. Even the descendants of the Olivieri brothers, who created the sandwich in the 1930s, are not in perfect agreement on the perfect cheesesteak. Thin-sliced meat is the norm, yet many Philadelphians prefer the meat shredded. Must the meat be beef or is a chicken cheesesteak a real thing? And of course, Cheez Whiz, a key feature of what many would call the default Philly cheesesteak, wasn't even invented until twenty years after the cheesesteak made its debut. The earliest sandwiches had provolone, though American is also a canonical choice. (Swiss is a no-no, as John Kerry learned in 2004.)

The vegan cheesesteak, of course, takes these variables to the farthest extreme possible, seeming to negate both halves of the compound word that describes the item. And maybe it does, but there's no reason vegans visiting Philadelphia shouldn't also get their chance to enjoy a cheesesteak in yet another variant form, especially given the growing number of venues around town that offer their own version.

The first vegan cheesesteak ever in Philly is shrouded in history, but a key pioneer in marketing such a sandwich consistently was Alfoncie Austin at Basic 4 Vegetarian in the Reading Terminal Market. As of this writing, Austin is the likeliest progenitor of the vegan cheesesteak as a regular menu item in Philadelphia (see "The Pre–'Vegan Scene' Days" in this volume). In the late 1990s and throughout the aughts, meat-free steak sandwiches began popping up here and there, with several Philadelphia bars leading the charge, some also offering soy cheese as time went on.

By 2010, I published my first "Top 10" list of veggie cheesesteaks in the *Daily News*, having determined that there were now at least ten instances in Philly of the item. Many of these were only vegan if you left off the cheese, but these joints—places like Govinda's, Sabrina's Cafe, and the Pub on Passyunk East (P.O.P.E.)—were pioneers in using seitan, soy crumbles, mushrooms, and other meat substitutes to normalize the notion of a meatless cheesesteak, which helped create conceptual space for the vegan version.

I had just filed my first *V for Veg* column in July 2011 when I started looking into doing a *Daily News*–sponsored contest that would provide exposure to many vegan (or would-be vegan) cheesesteaks while striving to name the best in town. In my conversations with the events people from our larger company, various formulations of the idea were proposed, considered (and sometimes tantalizingly close to happening), and eventually dropped for one regrettable reason or another. This dragged on for years.

Finally in late 2013, I resolved to make the event happen by doing the whole thing myself, and spring of 2014 saw the first instance of the Best Vegan Cheesesteak in Philly Contest, with the main *Daily News* contribution being the big "Daily News" banner as a backdrop and the features section in the paper to report developments and the winner.

First Year: 2014

There were a total of twenty nominees and three voting methods that year, with everyone allotted one vote per method (i.e., three total votes). One could email, tweet, and comment on the blog post "Tracking the Daily News Vegan Cheesesteak Contest." I collected all the votes in one master document that tracked each voter, when the vote came in, what number vote for a given venue it was, and other key information (including votes that were rejected, with the reason for rejecting them). With well over 300 votes in the span of the contest, this was a crazy-making endeavor, especially as I had publicly promised to furnish freshly updated contest totals on that blog post every 12 hours.

This obsessive approach was not, needless to say, replicated in subsequent years, but for that first year, I felt it was totally necessary to be sure our data integrity was impeccable, in case anyone who didn't win wanted to challenge the results, and in case the public in general might think it was a predetermined promotional stunt rather than a legitimate contest. For the finals, I came up with a double-blind judging system to keep results as objectively valid as possible. Meanwhile, there was considerable anxiety over whether we would have a finalist whose standard sandwich was not vegan.

As per the rules of the contest, nominees could be any meat-less, cheeseless sandwich offered as a "cheesesteak" on the venue's regular menu. But given that many of the rolls used for veggie cheesesteaks (including some "vegan" ones) contained whey and/ or animal-derived dough conditioners, most of the sandwiches competing were not 100 percent vegan. The rules stipulated that those being judged would have to be vegan through and through, so I knew there was a chance we'd have one sandwich competing in the finals that would have to provide an alternate version (on an alternate roll) for the top prize, which would be kind of weird, and I didn't know how well the enforcement of this provision would be received by the parties in question. I dreaded putting all this work into a project that might end in a public fiasco, reinforcing the meme that it's "too hard" to actually be vegan.

As it happened, though, our three finalists were all legit vegan sandwiches, and the final judging event at Grindcore House Cafe on March 18 was a well-attended, fun event that crowned Blackbird Pizzeria as the winner over finalists Hibiscus Cafe and Cantina Dos Segundos, a Mexican-themed bar whose entry, created specifically for the contest, was a vegan cheesesteak burrito. (The 2014 rules had no stipulation as to the format of the sandwich, but the 2015 rules sure did.)

Our judges that first year were Jonathan Bagot, who had pioneered vegan-cheesesteak cataloging with his listings on VeganJawn.com; Takia McClendon, who had helmed pop-up vegan soul-food events in and around Germantown; local vegan TV legend Christina Pirello; and Frank Olivieri Jr., the proprietor of Pat's Steaks and our sole nonvegan judge.

Finally the contest had come to fruition. But Blackbird's Mark Mebus had barely put his arms down after raising them for a triumphant "Whoo-hoo!" upon the announcement of the winner when I heard cries of "Just wait till next year!" My idea had been to find and name the best in town, but at that point I realized that this was something we could, and should, do every year.

Second Year: 2015

When we decided to come back and do the contest for a second year, I gave Blackbird the option of retiring as Winner Emeritus, with subsequent contestants all striving to be the "other" best vegan cheesesteaks in town, but Mebus wanted to be in the midst of it, especially since he felt Blackbird had improved its sandwich over the original version. That year, the contest was picked up as a philly.com initiative—no longer just *Daily News*—and the philly.com staff helped out by creating a cool logo and by setting up electronic voting on the site itself.

The second year of the contest proceeded more smoothly and with a slightly higher profile. Mebus and I appeared on *Good Day Philadelphia*, the morning show on Fox 29, where host Mike Jerrick acted out the boggling of the mind that the phrase "vegan cheesesteak" engenders while Mark assembled a sandwich. The whole event was TV-level superficial, but Mark and I collaborated to get an animal-conscious message through the noise.

With philly.com now handling the voting, the smooth ride for 2015 continued right up to the final judging event, held on March 20 at Weavers Way Co-op in the far-northwest Chestnut Hill section of Philadelphia. The distance from Center City didn't seem like that big a deal until a sudden first-day-of-spring snowstorm paralyzed traffic all across town. Our slated judges were Frank Olivieri Jr., Councilwoman Cindy Bass, Dr. Ana Negron, and Ed Coffin, a young vegan businessman and activist with Peace Advocacy Network.

By start time, Coffin was still waiting for a fallen tree to be removed from the main northwest artery, Lincoln Drive. Freya Dinshah of the American Vegan Society was tabling at the event and was conscripted to collaborate on an ad hoc Coffin-Dinshah judging team so that we could get started, with Coffin's tasting sample divided in two so he could have independent bites once he arrived, which he did about a third of the way through.

The logistical drama of making the event happen at all was soon superseded by the results: Blackbird was dethroned by new-comer Royal Tavern (another sandwich created for the contest, like the first-year burrito, by Mark McKinney, a chef contribut-ing to multiple restaurants), with the consolation that the winner was using Blackbird seitan. The vegan-friendly food truck Jerry's Kitchen came in third.

Afterward, McKinney noted that three out of five judges remarked positively on the inclusion of roasted mushrooms in Royal Tavern's entry, which "may have put me over the edge."

Third Year: 2016

With the contest now becoming a Philly "tradition," we decided to kick things up a proverbial notch and wound up at Union Trans-fer, the hottest music club in Center City, whose mostly vegetarian chief, Sean Agnew, convinced me that we should charge admission and have cheesesteak sampling as part of the event. This worked moderately well, except that a glitch in the voting platform led to closing electronic voting early, which screwed up some scheduling aspects, and also that Agnew departed for Africa before laying out the specific plans to accomplish this grander scheme.

I dived in and thought things were pretty well set up, but some last-minute changes—an employee injury that knocked out one venue planning to sample and a couple other less-well-explained last-minute bailing by a couple other venues—left us with the challenge of showing that this kind of citywide event could happen at a major entertainment spot and not be a fiasco. (Yes, again the "fiasco" specter loomed.)

In the end, we had only two contestant venues (The Abbaye, which finished fourth in the voting, and Frankie's on Fairview from the suburbs, one of the three finalists) giving out vegan cheesesteak samples, which meant long lines. There were plenty of other small missteps as well, but we cleared the bar of it not being a fiasco, a quality standard on which I hope to build in 2017.

In terms of contest specifics, Frankie's wound up placing behind Triangle Tavern (another new contest-inspired entry from Mark McKinney) and Blackbird Pizzeria, which regained the top spot it had ceded to McKinney the previous year. The judges were *Daily News* columnist/legend and token nonvegan Stu Bykofsky, former state representative (and longtime vegan) Babette Josephs, former Basic 4 manager Lisa Tynes, and Peace Advocacy Network activist Leila Vaughan (Frank Olivieri Jr. served as emcee for the event). They agreed that while Frankie's was a fun entry, the particular seasoning and processing of the seitan by Paul Carmine rendered it too much like a "chicken" cheesesteak. I had asked the judges to include their own notion of what the ideal "normal" cheesesteak was as one of the three criteria (along with flavor and texture), and apparently some—including, most vocally, Stu Bykofsky—felt a chicken cheesesteak was not a canonical variant.

We did get a chance with this contest to recognize Alfoncie Austin's pioneering work with Basic 4 Cafe, hoping to help today's hipster-vegan crowd grasp that the ease and relative normalcy of their present-day lifestyle is built on a foundation created by forward-looking hard-workers like Austin and her daughter Tynes. With Tynes as a judge and Austin as a guest of honor, we set aside a moment to thank both for helping build that foundation, which I considered a personal "win," justifying the existence of the contest beyond promoting this or that current business.

More Citywide Vegan Food Events

Throwing together the Union Transfer–size event pretty much on my own (other than some great assistance by Union Transfer staff) was, let's say, an even more educational experience than the first two years had been. There are many things that could have been done better—for example, overbooking venue participants so last-minute dropouts didn't decimate our food offering and having more stuff to do, see, hear, try, and so on right when doors opened—to make sure the ticket price and the experience of the participant matched up. Unfortunately, the chance to experience my off-the-cuff witticisms in person can only count for a certain percentage of an average ticket price.

As educational as it's been for me getting this citywide vegan event to a point of prominence and inevitability, I like to think it was also educational for the vegan community at large. With the standard correlation/causation caveat, it does seem worthy of note that since the occasion of the third annual cheesesteak contest in 2016, there have been quite a few citywide events that have had an explicitly vegan focus—stuff that had never happened before in Philadelphia.

In May, I attended the Vegan Mac and Cheese "Mac-Down" created by the V Marks the Shop team (who hope to open a vegan convenience store in Philly), and by the time of this writing, they had also launched the Vegan Pop Flea and the Philly Vegan Homecoming. At the same venue as the Mac and Cheese contest (the Rotunda in West Philly, site of the Veggie Cabarets) was June's Vegan Chef Lenka Brunch, and more vegan events will be happening there in late 2016.

This is not to ignore the increasing number of vegan-friendly events held at nonvegan venues in town. As this book went to press, Strangelove's bar announced a November Vegan Beer Dinner, a "five-course vegan feast paired with vegan beers" that's likely to be part of a trend.

The biggest Philly vegan food event held so far was at Sugarhouse Casino in August. The Sustainable Everyday Edibles and Drinkables (S.E.E.D.) Festival, which I emceed but did not help organize, was an all-vegan food-and-drink fest put on by a nonvegan team of beer-event promoters in a new, ritzy event space at Philly's only downtown casino.

This was an ambitious undertaking in the spirit of the cheesesteak contest, and I was happy to see how far Philly had come in citywide vegan events in just a few years. A complaint was that the amount of vegan food at the event was minimal, an effect of—surprise!—vegan venues agreeing to show up and then changing their minds for one reason or another, and I certainly sympathized when attendees raked the S.E.E.D. organizers over the coals for this. Less defensible was that one of the sampling vendors was giving out nonvegan food, a compromise the organizers admitted to making due to the low numbers of food tables showing up, and one brewer including tasting beers that contained honey. But like me, the organizers are listening and learning, and if anything, I can only expect more expansion of Philly-wide events showcasing tasty vegan food.

For the Animals

Philly is not just a great place for vegan eating; the city also has a history of animal activism and currently boasts multiple activist groups devoted to changing attitudes about animals, from street protests to festivals and entertainment-based events that raise awareness for vegan ideals.

History

It's worth noting that animal-friendly groups based in Philadelphia were at the forefront of nineteenth-century activism, spurred by the Bible Christians, for whom the abolition of slavery and the establishing of female suffrage were core goals. By the dawn of the twentieth century, though, vegetarianism had shifted from a moral imperative to a healthy lifestyle choice, and for many, there was a divorce of the two concepts of ethical eating and ethical living.

Ethics-based activism undoubtedly occurred through the early twentieth century, but it was somewhat under the radar as compared to the latter half. In 1957, Philadelphia served as the turning point for H. Jay Dinshah, who vowed to go vegan while standing on the corner of Front and Venango Streets after emerging from a tour of the Cross Brothers slaughterhouse.

Dinshah founded the American Vegan Society three years later in nearby Malaga, New Jersey, and began crusading across the country, helping bring together scattered and nascent vegan advocacy groups into a stronger network of information and promotion. To reach wider populations, Dinshah cofounded the North American Vegetarian Society in 1975, at first a vegetarian organization with strong vegan tendencies, then soon an all-vegan institution that nonetheless retained its more publicity-friendly name.

During this time, though there were groups around the Delaware Valley and elsewhere that were dedicated to the welfare of cats and dogs (the Pennsylvania Society for the Prevention of Cruelty to Animals [PSPCA] had been founded back in 1867), Philadelphia and South Jersey were generally not hubs of activism on behalf of animals from a vegan perspective.

In the 1980s, however, Philly saw one of the country's biggest animal-abuse cases (after the Silver Spring monkeys of 1981 in Maryland) involving our region's most prominent animal-rights thinker, Gary Francione. This was the closing of the University of Pennsylvania Baboon Lab that was headed by neurosurgeon Thomas Gennarelli.

As a sidebar to a *Philadelphia City Paper* cover-story profile, I talked with Francione in 2000 about these events that wound up at the epicenter of national animal-rights activism at the time. Here are some condensed excerpts from that chronicle:

> It's stuff you might see anywhere: College students smoke, joke, laugh, drop their utensils, complain about the dust, the grime and the administration. But the setting is the Head Injury lab at the University of Pennsylvania in the early '80s, and all of this is going on while they're holding and manipulating drugged and brain-damaged baboons. The baboons are being forcibly and precisely injured in the name of science, but the student research assistants act like they're working at Burger King.
>
> This footage is part of the 70 hours of videotapes which the experimenters took themselves and which were stolen from the lab on May 29, 1984.

The Animal Liberation Front, which claimed credit for the break-in and "liberation" of the tapes, got copies into the hands of PETA and its attorney, Gary Francione, who had recently accepted, but had not yet begun, a job as an assistant professor at Penn. The tapes were edited down into a 26-minute compilation of some of the worst, and most illegal, conduct, and it's still hard to watch.

It's unsettling enough to see students holding traumatized baboons and making jokes about the baboons' head wounds ("That's some part you've got there. He has the punk look.") and generally mocking them. ("He says, 'You're gonna rescue me from this, aren't you? Aren't you?'") But what's worse is the stuff that makes the whole enterprise unscientific: Non-sterile surgical conditions; constant smoking by the students (sometimes within a couple inches of incisions, and always in proximity of oxygen tanks); and the hammering of the metal plates off of the baboons' heads (polluting the data, which was supposed to measure injuries caused by shaking, not blows to the head). In other words, it's not just that animals were being abused, traumatized and taunted in the course of science—it's in the course of bad science.

The university, however, defended the research and refused to discontinue the experiments. In October 1984, PETA came to the University City Hilton to show their 26-minute compilation, *Unnecessary Fuss* (after a remark made by lab head Thomas Gennarelli). The showing was thronged by local media, and by law enforcement as well. The District Attorney's Office, headed by Ed Rendell, was very eager to ferret out the actual criminals who had stolen the tapes. So at the showing, according to Francione, "Anyone who answered 'yes' to the question 'Are you a member of PETA?' was handed a John Doe or Jane Doe subpoena to testify before a grand jury."

The police also wanted to confiscate all copies of the video and went to the Holiday Inn where Ingrid Newkirk was staying.

Francione reports, "There were at least 50 Philadelphia police officers looking for her." He found an internal stairwell that led to an unguarded exit, called her on the phone and described where it was. She left the room with the tapes and slipped into the stairwell just in time.

Newkirk says, "I remember being chased down the stairwell by people—I never found out if they were police or FBI or what—but they were people who were trying to seize the tape."

During the grand jury hearings, Francione represented many of the activists (including PETA head Alex Pacheco) who had been at the showing, over the District Attorney's objections that Francione was "one of them," part of the conspiracy to steal the tapes. Those hearings ended without any arrests, and the case is still open to this day.

Meanwhile, Francione collected internal Penn documents proving that the head injury lab had had other problems in the past, and submitted these to Congress, which led to congressional hearings on the lab in the spring of 1985.

PETA and their allies had followed the money to the National Institutes of Health. If Penn would not close the lab in the face of these and other clear violations (a summer 1984 USDA inspection cited 74 infractions), it was up to the NIH to cut off its funding. Instead, in the summer of 1985, the NIH increased the lab's grant, as if in defiance. On July 15, 1985, a hundred animal activists occupied Building 31-B of the NIH, refusing to leave until the lab was shut down. They fully expected to be arrested, but the authorities were unprepared for this tactic, and weren't sure how to proceed.

The sit-in stretched over four days. Francione, who represented the activists, was allowed in and out of the building as a negotiator. Finally, on the fourth day, HHS Secretary Margaret Heckler, who had now seen the tape, ordered the NIH to withdraw funding and close the lab. The university was sanctioned, and Gennarelli was forbidden to do any more research with apes.

> Said Francione, "It felt good to win by saying no to a system that was corrupt."

This was the biggest activist event for Philadelphia in terms of impact and media attention on the national stage, but there were other campaigns that were more localized.

In the late 1980s, an increased attention to the problem of carriage horses ferrying tourists on streets around the historic Old City area was addressed with large organized protests, which would continue on and off under the auspices of different groups up to this day. Progress on this has been frustrating for vegans: the industry persists with only minor regulatory strictures having been achieved via the city council (e.g., high-temperature prohibitions and housing), even as many tourists assume this cutesy "historical" and "traditional" industry dates back further than its actual start during the American Bicentennial in 1976.

Meanwhile, groups focusing on cats and dogs expanded their attention from simple spay-and-neuter programs (the national group Friends of Animals was an early pioneer and briefly ran a chapter in Philadelphia) to include the rescue of different kinds of animals and efforts to rehouse them (e.g., RatChick Rat Rescue). Mobilization for Animals worked in this area early on, while also organizing demonstrations. And while Club Veg, which had a chapter in Philadelphia for several years, focused mostly on food activism, it also addressed animal issues and was part of an activist consortium that put together the proanimal "Better Living Festival" at The Ethical Society in 2000.

Philadelphia is also the home of what's known as America's oldest zoo, and this institution has drawn its share of rebuke and ongoing protest by animal activists. One event that shocked even those apathetic about animal interests was the primate-house 1995 fire that killed 23 great apes. This tragic accident (as well as others at this zoo and elsewhere), along with an increasing understanding of the need for large animals to have room to roam, likely helped boost the message of groups such as Friends of Philly Zoo Elephants, whose campaign urging the zoo to close the elephant exhibit finally paid off in 2006, with the zoo going elephant-free.

The head of Friends of Philly Zoo Elephants, Marianne Bessey, was also involved in the most recent animal-activism case to receive national attention. In June of 2011, a cow escaped from the Madina slaughterhouse in Upper Darby and roamed the streets of the Philly suburb long enough to garner the attention of local news before being recaptured by police. As often happens, the individuality of the animal pulled at the public's heartstrings (in a way that the enormous number of similar animals being slaughtered does not seem to), and in the midst of an uproar about returning the cow to the slaughterhouse, Bessey and fellow activist Elissa Katz stepped in.

Eventually they assembled a coalition that grew to include Moein Khawaja of the Council on American Islamic Relations as well as the Pennsylvania Department of Agriculture and even Governor Tom Corbett (who issued a "pardon"), and after a two-week quarantine, the cow, now named Kayli, wound up traveling to Woodstock Farm Animal Sanctuary to become one of the organization's most beloved poster children of what founder Jenny Brown's book termed *The Lucky Ones*.

Meanwhile, in less confrontational activist endeavors, the group Public Eye: Artists for Animals organized many events bringing an animal-friendly message to the Philly public, ranging from musical get-togethers to art gallery exhibits. Some of the most prominent were held at the Rotunda in University City: the Veggie Cabaret (2007; featuring nationally syndicated vegan cartoonist Dan "Bizarro" Piraro), Veggie Cabaret II (2009; also featuring Piraro), and Carnivores Anonymous (2011; I was also involved in these three productions).

Present Day

Nowadays, if you're in Philly and want to participate in a demonstration or other event, or if you want to get information related to animal advocacy, here are some of the top groups that are making things happen:

Animal Activists of Philly

This group has evolved out of Friends of Philly Zoo Elephants and continues to hold demonstrations at the Philadelphia Zoo. In 2016, the group launched a new campaign called "Change the Zoo," encouraging the zoo not to close but to convert to a sanctuary model. It also protests circuses that use animals and animal-breeding institutions.

www.meetup.com/Animal-Activists-of-Philly

CARE

Compassion for Animals, Respect for the Environment (CARE) is one of the oldest organizations devoted to animals in the Philly area, founded in 1991. Though its members pursue more direct animal activism on various fronts, which CARE facilitates, the tentpole in terms of activism for this group has historically been its annual vegan festival held in Chester County.

www.chestercountycare.com

The Humane League

An earlier incarnation, Hugs for Puppies, focused on protesting animals used for medical research. After rebranding, The Humane League (THL) has successfully encouraged many food businesses in Philly to add stickers to their doors notifying customers of "Vegan Options Inside" and in 2013 got city council to officially endorse Meatless Mondays. Now with a national reach, THL works largely on campaigns to improve the welfare of factory-farmed animals.

www.thehumaneleague.com

Kind Institute

A relatively new initiative cofounded by Maria Pandolfi of RatChick Rat Rescue with the support of Lenka Zivkovic, a Philly vegan chef who blossomed into an activist and organizer, the Kind Institute works in the vein of Public Eye (which ceased when leader Lisa Levinson moved to California) on a smaller (or at least younger) scale, focusing on humane education in artistic and craft-based after-school programs in and around the Point Breeze neighborhood.

www.kindinstitute.org

PAN

Peace Advocacy Network (PAN), which has also expanded to other cities along the East Coast, focuses on intersectional issues, placing animal interests in a broader societal campaign that includes racial, gender, and sexual-orientation issues. For many years, in multiple Delaware Valley locations, PAN has run a thirty-day program called the Vegan Pledge, in which nonvegan participants learn about veganism and vegan living (and receive free vegan food and mentoring) for thirty days of pledged animal-free eating.

www.peaceadvocacynetwork.org

Other Sites and Sights

While you're in Philadelphia, you want to take every opportunity to sample the vegan scene, but you can't eat the *entire* time. So you'll want to work up an appetite by seeing the sights and taking in some nonculinary Philly culture.

In addition to such well-known mainstays as the Liberty Bell, Independence Hall, Valley Forge, and the Rocky Steps—better known as the entrance to the Philadelphia Museum of Art—there are many fun places around town to see that aren't as well known on the national front. Here are just a few of them.

Longwood Gardens
1001 Longwood Rd., Kennett Square, PA
(610) 388-1000

For another commune-with-nature experience that is, in this case, more carefully cultivated, this expanse of gardens, woodlands, and meadows across 1,077 acres is a good place to wander at a relaxed pace and soak up some natural beauty in splendiferous, colorful diversity. The lush conservatory is especially remarkable. Longwood Gardens hosts many horticultural and performing arts events each year, including flower shows, gardening demonstrations and courses, and children's programs, as well as musical theater and fountain shows. It's a ways outside the border of Philadelphia but well worth devoting an afternoon.

Mummers Museum
1100 S. 2nd St.
(215) 336-3050

The Mummers are a totally Philly institution, mostly blue-collar tough guys who dress up in frilly, fancy clothes (some in women's garb) on New Year's Day to parade up Broad Street playing banjoes (and other portable instruments) in a glitzy metropolitan riff on the ancient tradition of mumming. The museum boasts costumes, oral histories, video and audio archives, and even an exhibit to teach anyone how to "strut."

Mutter Museum
19 S. 22nd St.
(215) 563-3737

This looks and sounds similar to the previous entry but could hardly be more distinct. With twenty thousand artifacts of medical science, there are few museums more casually macabre than this one. It showcases such fun specimens as diseased and enlarged organs, abnormal body parts preserved in fluid, skeletal formations, and more fascinating specimens, plus historic equipment from Madame Curie and Dr. Benjamin Rush. One of the most notable items is the death cast of the "original" Siamese twins, Chang and Eng, whose autopsy was performed at the Mutter Museum.

Philadelphia History Museum at the Atwater Kent
15 S. 7th St.
(215) 685-4830

There's no shortage of historic museums in the area around Independence Mall, but this one a block away is special. It's the original site of the Franklin Institute science museum (also a fun visit but one most people hear about), a building owned by A. Atwater Kent, a wealthy inventor who manufactured early radios in Philadelphia. Not surprisingly, among the 100,000 objects in the museum are plenty associated with radio and other technology, but the collection also includes original prints, paintings, photographs, and other Philly-centric items dating from the 1680s to the present day.

Philadelphia's Magic Gardens
1020 South St.
(215) 733-0390

When people ask me what they can see in Philly that's off the beaten path but totally worth it, I send them to this one-of-a-kind attraction created by Isaiah Zagar, one of the team of counterculture entrepreneurs responsible for the "South Street Renaissance" of the early 1980s. Known around town (especially in neighborhoods near Old City) for his mosaic murals made from broken tiles, mirrors, glass bottles, and other odd-size objects, Zagar began covering a vacant lot with such mosaics in the 1990s, eventually creating a crazy-colorful, dizzying multifloor tribute to boundless artistic creativity that, after complicated legal machinations, evolved into a nonprofit organization offering site tours, art activities, workshops, concerts, and exhibitions.

Rodin Museum
2151 Benjamin Franklin Pkwy.
(215) 763-8100

Sandwiched in between the heavy hitters at either end of the Benjamin Franklin Parkway—that is, the Philadelphia Museum of Art to the west and the Barnes Foundation Museum to the east—the Rodin Museum houses a great collection of works (the largest outside of Paris) by the nineteenth-century French sculptor, including the *Gates of Hell* at the entrance and, out front pondering the parkway, one of a handful of versions Auguste Rodin did of *The Thinker*.

Wissahickon Creek in Fairmount Park

No address or phone here, but this creek that meets the Schuylkill River at Ridge Avenue and Lincoln Drive has miles of bucolic paths for walking and biking, including a long stretch known as Forbidden Drive, a road-sized path for pedestrians and cyclists only that runs parallel to the creek. It's pretty common knowledge that Fairmount Park is the largest park within the limits of any city in the United States, and the portions of the park that stretch along the Schuylkill down into the Philadelphia Museum of Art area are also quite nice, but this northwest area is a gem of low-key Zen.

Guidebook

Guidebook Notes

Listings in this book comprise places that are relatively certain to have something expressly vegan for a hungry Philly tourist or resident. As that set of restaurants and bars, happily, is constantly growing, this cannot be a comprehensive list of every venue with vegan options.

My emphasis was to try to include places that are most tied to the vegan community, both longtime stalwarts and fascinating newcomers, and that had either a great quantity of items or a noteworthy approach, at least from my own perspective. But readers are encouraged to keep their eyes open for any that weren't yet on my radar and let me know about them (vforveg@phillynews.com).

In addition to these individually listed venues, look for smoothie/juice bars, hoagie shops, water ice stands, Asian restaurants (especially Chinese, Indian, and Vietnamese) and places based on other non-Western cuisines, and veg-friendly chain restaurants for vegan eating opportunities. Be aware that hoagie rolls at some nonvegan establishments may or may not be strictly vegan depending on what kind of dough stabilizers are used in a given batch. Vegan restaurants, so far as I have found, use 100 percent vegan rolls. (Some nonvegan places also do expressly carry vegan rolls; they'll tell you so if you ask.)

These listings are divided into large geographical categories. Greater Center City is defined as the area from South Street up to Girard Avenue, from the Delaware River to the Schuylkill. South of that is the South Philly area. North of that is the Northeast/ Northwest area. Across the Schuylkill from Center City is West Philadelphia. Notable vegan-friendly venues from the general area are included in the suburbs section. There are also a handful of venues that are non-site-specific.

Within each geographical section, vegan restaurants are listed first alphabetically, followed by vegan-friendly restaurants also listed alphabetically. Those of the latter categorized as "Very Vegan-Friendly" are often vegetarian or near-vegan, but not always—the key is that they have a healthy collection of different kinds of vegan offerings. If there are only two or three options but the place is still worth noting, the venue "Has Vegan Items."

The price range is divided into three pretty standard levels. One dollar sign means a particular bargain or low-priced menu, usually in a very basic, no-frills setting; two is a moderate, main-stream level; and three indicates a place where you're paying for a higher level of cuisine and/or experience.

In order to give interested and hungry readers an idea of the cuisine involved, each listing has some examples of vegan items the venue has offered. Most of these were obtained via interviews with management, though a few were filled in from other sources, including many personal visits. Though great effort was under-taken to gather more permanent menu items, restaurant menus are constantly shifting, and this book makes no guarantee that any one item will be on a given menu at a given time.

Top Ten Must-Trys

Let's say you're in town for just a day or two, or are otherwise limited in how much of Philly's vegan scene you can sample. What are the places you'll want to prioritize if possible, the most archetypally "Philly vegan" of all the restaurants you might patronize? With the caveat that there are plenty of other great and iconic choices with fantastic food, here is my own Top Ten list—along with an indicator of which section you'll find them in—of 13 Philly-specific venues you simply must try to get to. All of these are 100 percent vegan, except Govinda's, which includes an option of dairy mozzarella.

- Blackbird Pizzeria (Center City)
- Govinda's Gourmet to Go (Center City)
- Grindcore House Cafe (South Philly)
- Miss Rachel's Pantry (South Philly)
- HipCityVeg (Center City; University City)
- The Nile (Northeast/Northwest)
- Sprig & Vine (Suburbs)
- Vedge (Center City)
- V Street (Center City)
- Wiz Kid (Center City)

Guidebook Listings

Greater Center City

Vegan

Bar Bombón

Category:	Vegan
Price Range:	$$
Favorite Eats:	EMPANADAS—Choice of leek, mushroom, and currant or "chorizo"
	BUFFALO CAULIFLOWER TACOS—Refried black beans, avocado, green goddess dressing, and mirepoix
	CUBANO CLUB—Grilled chicken breast, smoked tempeh, mustard aioli, dill pickles, shredded lettuce, and tomatoes
Comments:	Bar Bombón is a tribute to Puerto Rico's tropically cool open bars, at first opening with a mock-meats-heavy lineup but recently expanding the number of creative vegetable dishes, all touching somehow on the overarching San Juan theme.
Contact:	133 S. 18th St.
	(267) 606-6612
	www.barbombon.com

Blackbird Pizzeria

Category:	Vegan
Price Range:	$
Favorite Eats:	PIZZAS—"Haymaker" is the top seller: seitan sausage, red onions, garlic butter, tomato sauce, Daiya cheese, and fresh oregano WINGS—Root Beer BBQ is especially good CHEESESTEAK—Won Best Vegan Cheesesteak in Philly in 2014 and again in 2016
Comments:	Blackbird is a pioneer in vegan fast food in Philadelphia, having opened in 2010 and setting the trend for vegan pizza, among other things. The classic neighborhood-pizza-joint feel complements the animal-free dedication and, in its early years, hard-charging grindcore music (since mellowed).
Contact:	507 S. 6th St. (215) 625-6660 http://blackbirdpizzeria.com

Charlie Was a Sinner

Category:	Vegan
Price Range:	$$
Favorite Eats:	ZUCCHINI "CRAB CAKE" SLIDER—Old Bay remoulade BUCATINI AND "MEATBALLS"—Fra diavolo with basil KOREAN-STYLE FRIED TOFU—Spicy glaze, black sesame, and garden pickles
Comments:	This atmospheric, moodily lit vegan bar on the outskirts of the Gayborhood has won adherents with creatively rethought dishes and offerings like

"Our Ricotta," with agave, black peppercorn, and olive oil.

Contact:	131 S. 13th St.
	(267) 758-5372
	www.charliewasasinner.com

HipCityVeg—Rittenhouse

Category:	Vegan
Price Range:	$$
Favorite Eats:	CRISPY HIPCITY RANCH—Gardein patty with a peppercorn-ranch dressing, pickles, lettuce, tomato, and onion on whole-wheat roll
	PHILLYSTEAK—Pulled seitan steak, grilled onion, mushroom, lettuce, tomato, and organic ketchup on a whole-wheat long roll
	ZIGGY BURGER—Classic burger with organic smoked tempeh and special sauce
	UDON NOODLE SALAD—Spicy glazed chick'n with sprouts, arugula, carrot, cabbage, daikon, scallions, peanuts, and Chinese black bean dressing
	GROOTHIE—Green smoothie with organic apples, organic leafy greens, bananas, and seasonal fruit
Comments:	This vegan fast-food spot opened in March 2012 and quickly became a favorite lunch spot for Rittenhouse Square–area workers and residents. Cory Booker specifically mentioned HipCity and its "line down the block" as an indicator of people's interest in eating "good vegan food." From day one, the most popular sandwich has been the Crispy HipCity Ranch, and HipCity reminds you that "you can also choose to toss

the chick'n patty in buffalo sauce to spice it up!"
In addition to the healthful Groothie and sweet
potato fries, HCV also offers chocolate vegan
milkshakes and other seasonal shakes.

Contact: 127 S. 18th St.
             (215) 278-7605
             www.hipcityveg.com

HipCityVeg—S. Broad Street

Contact: 121 S. Broad St.
             See details above

Mi Lah

Category: Vegan

Price Range: $$

Favorite Eats: PAN SEARED RAVIOLIS—Cashew nut cream, truffle
                  oil, roasted cauliflower, and pepper topped with
                  almond slice
                  INDONESIAN ROLLS—Carrots, seitan, mushrooms,
                  and celery wrapped in crispy rice paper and served
                  with basil-avocado sauce
                  SHIITAKE-TRUFFLE OIL CAKE—Topped with
                  Mexican chili stew

Comments: Mi Lah long had a presence in the heart of
                  Center City but decamped a few years back for
                  the 'burbs—namely, Ambler, up Route 309.
                  This new location, set to open just below the
                  intersection of 3rd and South Streets after this
                  book goes to press, is said to be all-vegan.

Contact: www.milahvegetarian.com

New Harmony

Category:	Vegan
Price Range:	$
Favorite Eats:	ORANGE BEEF—Chopped, battered, and fried soy "beef" strips coated in a spicy sweet orange-flavored chili sauce, which caramelizes to a glaze GENERAL TSO'S CHICKEN—Deep-fried soy "chicken" seasoned with ginger, garlic, sesame oil, scallions, and hot chili peppers, served with steamed broccoli SCALLION PANCAKES—Non-leavened, salty flatbread infused with oil and minced scallions; also available in a spinach variety
Comments:	One of the handful of true vegan pioneer restaurants that are still around, New Harmony merits a stop for any visitor interested in an authentic Philly vegan experience—or anyone who just enjoys a tasty variety of animal-free food. A pan-Asian menu of soups, sauces, mock meats, nuts, grains, and fresh vegetables is tweaked and combined in a dizzying number of combinations, prepared simply but with care.
Contact:	135 N. 9th St. (215) 627-4520 https://www.facebook.com/New-Harmony-Vegetarian-Restaurant-192359379755

Plantpure Cafe

Category:	Vegan
Price Range:	$
Favorite Eats:	VEGGIES BOWL—Served over rice and quinoa or roasted potatoes, with soy curls, seitan, or tofu

and four options of sauces: red coconut curry, Jerk peanut, teriyaki, or creamy mushroom
Sandwiches or Wraps—Varieties such as Banh Mi, PlantSteak, and Baked Falafel
Salad Bar—Includes lots of fresh veggies and many dressings, all oil-free

Comments: Set to open as this book is going to press, this reincarnation of the old Vgë Café of Bryn Mawr as a nearly oil-free whole-foods plant-based fast-food joint has all of Philly's vegan community watching from the edge of their seats.

Contact: 1115 Walnut St.

P.S. & Co.

Category: Vegan

Price Range: $$$

Favorite Eats: Organic Chocolate Chip Quinoa Pancakes—Served with mushroom bacon and maple syrup
Burmese Sprouted Chickpea Curry—Served with brown rice and massaged kale
Mac and Cheese—Sweet potato pine nut sauce with brown rice pasta

Comments: Growing out of a cold-pressed organic juice business, this eclectic, offbeat cafe offers plenty of signature juice and smoothie items and also pastries like Banana Chocolate Bread, salads and bowls like Garden Pad Thai Stir Fry, and sandwiches like the Black Bean Burger and Portobello Mozzarella Focaccia Sandwich, plus tofu scramble, brownies, coconut yogurt, and miso soup.

Contact:	1706 Locust St.
	(215) 985-1706
	www.puresweets.com

Sweet Freedom Bakery

Category:	Vegan
Price Range:	$$
Favorite Eats:	MAGIC BAR—Shortbread crust with chocolate glaze and coconut flakes
	SALTED CARAMEL CUPCAKES
	SAMOA COOKIES—Caramel and toasted coconut
Comments:	This bakery carved out the niche of allergen-free, gluten-free baked goods in 2010. In addition to over-the-counter cupcakes, donuts, and other treats, Sweet Freedom does custom orders of cakes and pies. Originally some items included honey, but a rep assured me that all items are now honey-free.
Contact:	1424 South St.
	(215) 545-1899
	www.sweetfreedombakery.com

V Street

Category:	Vegan
Price Range	$$
Favorite Eats:	LANGOS—Mini-pizza-like appetizer featuring soft bread topped with smoked Chioggia beets, dill, and sauerkraut remoulade
	CAULIFLOWER "65"—Whipped dal, mint chutney, and curry hot sauce

KOREAN FRIED TEMPEH TACOS—Radish kimchee, grilled tomato, and sriracha Thousand Island

Comments: Really, it's a fool's errand trying to pick out highlights from this menu because everything is singular and fantastic. The BBQ Trumpet Mushrooms, Dan Dan Noodles, or Peruvian Fries could as easily have been placed under the "Favorite Eats." Note that in addition to being slightly less expensive and more casual than its big sister, Vedge, this bar's menu tends toward items that are spicier, the better to wash down with the vegan craft beers, wines, and creative cocktails. Also note that V Street will undergo an overhaul at the end of 2016, adding a noodle bar (and likely dropping some menu items) with the opening of Wiz Kid in a conjoined space next door.

Contact: 126 S. 19th St.
(215) 278-7943
http://vstreetfood.com

Vedge

Category:	Vegan
Price Range:	$$$
Favorite Eats:	GRILLED SEITAN—This has been on the menu from the earliest Horizons days, but it is often tweaked slightly by the restless chef. Current lineup includes horseradish, pickled celery, and charred kohlrabi slaw
	SHAVED BRUSSELS SPROUTS—Served with smoked grain mustard (Don't worry if you didn't like Brussels sprouts as a child—these will make you a convert.)

RUTABAGA FONDUE—Served with soft pretzel and pickle

Comments: You've likely heard of this place, which no one would deny has become Philadelphia's signature vegan restaurant; it was voted to have the "Best Food" out of all the restaurants in town by five thousand Zagat readers. It does get busy, though, so if you're planning a visit to Philly and thinking of trying it for dinner, make a reservation once you get to the end of this sentence. Otherwise, there are often seats at the bar, especially if you get there early, and there is a separate happy hour menu that includes a few more casual ("V Street"–style) appetizers and sandwiches. Be sure to try some of the house-made ice creams overseen by Kate Jacoby, often involving wacky mashups such as jalapeño and basil that somehow work together perfectly.

Contact: 1221 Locust St.
(215) 320-7500
www.vedgerestaurant.com

Vegan Tree

Category:	Vegan
Price Range:	$
Favorite Eats:	VEGAN TREE WRAP—White tortilla wrap with sweet and sour patties, tofu, red pepper, cooked onion, and black rice CHICKPEA AVOCADO SALAD—Greens, chickpeas, black beans, avocado, carrots, green pepper, red pepper, and cucumbers with ginger fruit dressing

VEGAN TREE SPECIAL SMOOTHIE—Kale, avocado, banana, Fuji apple, ginger, and organic soy milk

Comments: An eclectic little diner right in the heart of the South Street area, Vegan Tree boasts a wide range of options that also includes sushi, bubble tea, soy milkshakes, chocolate cake, and a vegan cheesesteak.

Contact: 742 South St.
(215) 454-2898
www.742vegantree.com

Wiz Kid I—Whole Foods

Category: Vegan

Price Range: $$

Favorite Eats: WIZ KID—Mushroom steak sandwich with "long hots" (Italian peppers) and rutabaga wiz

Comments: The newest effort from Philly vegan superstars Rich Landau and Kate Jacoby is opening as this book goes to press. This location is a counter within the Pennsylvania Avenue Whole Foods, offering a more limited selection than the Rittenhouse location (see the following).

Contact: 2101 Pennsylvania Ave.

Wiz Kid II—Rittenhouse

Category: Vegan

Price Range: $$

Favorite Eats: WIZ KID—Mushroom steak sandwich with "long hots" (Italian peppers) and rutabaga wiz

KFT—Korean fried tempeh sandwich
VEGAN ICE CREAMS

Comments: The newest effort from Philly vegan superstars Rich Landau and Kate Jacoby is opening as this book goes to press, offering a small menu of quick-serve items anchored by a signature vegan cheesesteak. This location will offer a few more selections than the Whole Foods counter (see the previous entry).

Contact: 124 S. 19th St.

Vegan-Friendly

The Abbaye

Category: Very Vegan-Friendly

Price Range: $$

Favorite Eats: SEITAN VEGAN WINGS
SEITAN CHEESESTEAK—Available with vegan cheese and vegan mayo, a frequent top contender in the Best Vegan Cheesesteak in Philly contest
AUTUMN VEGGIE BURGER—Brown rice, and pepper pear relish on brioche

Comments: This beloved Northern Liberties bar was ahead of the vegan-wing trend and has hosted the annual Vegan Wing Bowl. It was one of the key stops in my vegan-food bar-hopping night with Joe Sixpack, as chronicled in *V for Veg*. For those pairing at home, I washed down the vegan wings with a Troeg's Perpetual IPA.

Contact: 637 N. 3rd St.
(215) 627-6711
www.theabbaye.net

Agno Grill

Category:	Has Vegan Items
Price Range:	$$
Favorite Eats:	Coconut-Based Vegan Rice Pudding
Comments:	This restaurant allows customers to build their own wraps, salads, and bowls with many vegan components, including oven-baked falafel. It also features roasted cauliflower, cucumber-tomato salad, and quinoa tabbouleh, plus vegan cookies (sesame tahini and/or cherry walnut).
Contact:	2104 Chestnut St.
	(267) 858-4590
	www.agnogrill.com

Belgian Cafe

Category:	Very Vegan-Friendly
Price Range:	$$
Favorite Eats:	Seitan Wings—Served with a choice of three different vegan sauces
	Tacos—Served with Seitan Chorizo
	Homemade Veggie Burger—Served with mushrooms, carrots, and chickpeas
Comments:	This is one of Philly's bars going the extra mile to provide something interesting for vegans. The vegetable risotto can also be made as a vegan dish.
Contact:	601 N. 21st St.
	(215) 235-3500
	www.thebelgiancafe.com

Cantina Dos Segundos

Category:	Has Vegan Items
Price Range:	$$
Favorite Eats:	VEGAN-CHEESESTEAK BURRITO—Seitan carne asada, Daiya mozzarella, fried yucca, chipotle onions, lettuce, and smoked mushroom ketchup
	CHIMICHANGA—Fried flour tortilla with Mexican rice and refried beans (vegan cheese and vegan beef option)
	TRES PAPAYAS—Green papaya, papaya escabeche, avocado, red onion, cilantro, and papaya seed vinaigrette (can be ordered with seitan)
Comments:	One of Mark McKinney's signature vegan-enhanced bar menus, Cantina Dos Segundos made a name for itself in the vegan world in 2014 by introducing the Vegan-Cheesesteak Burrito, which was a finalist in that year's Best Vegan Cheesesteak in Philly Contest. With large windows open to the sidewalk in warm weather, the cantina has become a fixture in Northern Liberties. In addition to the food previously mentioned, it also offers vegan nachos.
Contact:	931 N. 2nd St.
	(215) 629-0500
	www.cantinadossegundos.com

Erewhan

Category:	Has Vegan Items
Price Range:	$$
Favorite Eats:	THAI-RIFFIC GOLDEN TOFU—Served with sweet and sour sauce and crushed peanut

CURRY GARDEN (PAD PAK KANG DANG)—Sautéed tofu and vegetables simmered in coconut milk and red curry sauce

TOM YUM RICE NOODLE SOUP (TOFU)—
Served with lemongrass, lime juice, Thai chili, mushrooms, and choice of rice noodle or bean thread noodles

Comments: This small Thai restaurant has both vegan menu items and many vegetarian options that can be veganized.

Contact: 123 S. 23rd St.
(215) 567-2542
www.erawanphilly.com

Franklin Fountain

Category: Has Vegan Items

Price Range: $

Favorite Eats: ICE CREAM—Vanilla or chocolate ice cream cones always available in vegan versions

MILKSHAKES—Blending vegan ice cream and either almond milk or coconut milk

CARAMEL APPLE PIE SHAKE—A milkshake with hot elements

Comments: Franklin Fountain was an early adopter of vegan inclusion. Vegan strawberry ice cream is often available but not always; nondairy seasonal flavors rotate in, such as pumpkin and apple cider in the fall and peppermint stick in the winter. During cold months, this venue also serves vegan (coconut-based) hot chocolate. The Fountain also has fancy ices—lemon is always available.

Contact: 116 Market St.
(215) 627-1899
www.franklinfountain.com

Govinda's Gourmet to Go

Category:	Very Vegan-Friendly
Price Range:	$
Favorite Eats:	CHICKEN CHEESESTEAK—Soy chicken, rainbow peppers, and soy cheese served on long roll or in a wrap, Philly's signature vegan chicken cheesesteak
	SLOPPY JOE—Soy-based favorite also available on a roll or in a wrap
	SMOOTHIES—From the juice bar
Comments:	Originally an adjunct to a fine-dining vegetarian restaurant, GTG outlived that era with a diner-style fast-food corner spot at Broad and South. The chicken cheesesteak has been a well-loved contender in the Best Vegan Cheesesteak in Philly Contest. Nearly everything on the menu is vegan, except for the option of dairy-based mozzarella cheese on sandwiches. Yeah, I know.
Contact:	1408 South St. (215) 545-5452 www.govindasvegetarian.com

Govinda's in Bakhti Garden

Category:	Very Vegan-Friendly
Price Range:	$$
Favorite Eats:	Pizza

Comments:	Just opened in late 2016, this overhaul of the main Govinda's concept presents a vegan, kosher-certified organic buffet with offerings both hot and raw, as well as a pizza counter selling both regular and vegan pizzas (Daiya cheese).
Contact:	1408 South St. (215) 545-5452 www.govindasvegetarian.com

Honeygrow

Category:	Very Vegan-Friendly
Price Range:	$$
Favorite Eats:	ROASTED TOMATO MISO KALE SALAD—Roasted tomato miso dressing, green kale, organic roasted spicy tofu, apples, carrots, roasted beets, red onions, radishes, and sesame sticks RED COCONUT CURRY STIR-FRY—Red coconut curry sauce, rice noodles, organic roasted spicy tofu, pineapples, jalapeños, bean sprouts, scallions, and cilantro CREATE YOUR OWN STIR-FRY WITH SESAME GARLIC SAUCE—Organic roasted spicy tofu, choice of vegetables and garnish, and choice of brown rice, rice noodles, Boston lettuce cups, or our freshly made whole-wheat noodles
Comments:	Honeygrow is based on a stir-fry or noodle-bowl model, so there are plenty of components to include or leave out to create your favorite food.
Contact:	110 S. 16th St. (215) 279-7724 www.honeygrow.com

Honey's Sit 'N Eat

Category:	Has Vegan Items
Price Range:	$$
Favorite Eats:	TOFU SCRAMBLE—Served with spicy veg sausage, spinach, mushrooms, and grilled potatoes HOUSE-MADE VEGGIE BURGER—Vegan if ordered on vegan bread instead of brioche VEGAN ENFRIJOLADAS—Beans, tofu, and microgreen salad
Comments:	This diner-style venue emphasizes good ol' home-style American fare but puts an interesting spin on many items, with many veganizable dishes via the omission of the dairy component.
Contact:	800 N. 4th St. (215) 925-1150 www.honeyssitneat.com

Khyber Pass Pub

Category:	Very Vegan-Friendly
Price Range:	$$
Favorite Eats:	VEGAN BBQ PULLED PORK SANDWICH—Spicy vinegar-ketchup barbecue sauce and coleslaw GRILLED VEGAN SAUSAGE—Seitan sausage patties, lettuce, roasted poblanos, red onion, pickles, creole mustard, and vegan mayo VEGAN FRIED CHICKEN PO' BOY—Breaded seitan on long roll with lettuce, tomato, pickles, mayo, and creole mustard
Comments:	One of Mark McKinney's signature vegan-enhanced bar menus, Khyber Pass was transformed from a seedy live-music joint to a dining hotspot

and set the bar for creative vegan pub food with its Southern-inflected selections. It also features fun finger food such as vegan buttered popcorn.

Contact:	56 S. 2nd St.
	(215) 238-5888
	www.khyberpasspub.com

King of Falafel

Category:	Very Vegan-Friendly
Price Range:	$
Favorite Eats:	FALAFEL SANDWICH—Served in a wrap with lettuce, tomato, onions, and tahini
Comments:	This entry is for any folks who find themselves wandering around the environs of City Hall on a weekday, hoping for something both vegan and authentically Philly. The King of Falafel food truck is legendary for its falafel sandwiches (vegan if no tzatziki sauce), which are usually offered in a wrap and are always satisfying.
Contact:	16th St. and JFK Blvd.
	https://twitter.com/kfalafel

Mama's Vegetarian

Category:	Very Vegan-Friendly
Price Range:	$
Favorite Eats:	FALAFEL PLATTER—Served with pita, hummus, and assorted pickles
	VEGAN LATKE PLATTER—Two patties served with hummus and vegetables
	BAKLAVA—Honey-free

Comments: An almost-vegan establishment, Mama's still includes a couple dishes with egg. However, Philly vegans recognize Mama's as something close to the best falafel in town. It is closed on Saturdays.

Contact: 18 S. 20th St.
(215) 751-0477
www.mamasvegetarian.com

Monk's Cafe

Category: Has Vegan Items

Price Range: $$

Favorite Eats: PORTOBELLO SANDWICH—Dressed with hummus or black bean dip
ROASTED SPAGHETTI SQUASH—Served with grilled artichoke
SEITAN STEAK SANDWICH—Grilled seitan on long roll with onions and peppers

Comments: Monk's is a Belgian-themed bar/restaurant close to the Kimmel Center and other Center City attractions. As of this writing, Monk's only offers nonvegan cheese with the steak sandwich, but it's good without cheese. (It was at Monk's, eating that very item, that I decided to get to work on a citywide vegan cheesesteak contest.)

Contact: 264 S. 16th St.
(215) 545-7005
www.monkscafe.com

Mugshots

Category:	Very Vegan-Friendly
Price Range:	$
Favorite Eats:	VEGAN CHAIN GANG SANDWICH—Served with hummus and veggies VEGAN BLT—Smoked tempeh, lettuce, tomato, and soy mayo FRUIT PLATTER—Varies with the season, mixing local with exotic
Comments:	In its earliest incarnation, this chain featured a decor based around its name, but the more casual version is nice in its own way. In addition to the vegan snacks and sandwiches on offer, coffees, teas, smoothies, and juices are complemented by bagels with vegan cream cheese and vegan baked goods.
Contact:	1925 Fairmount Ave. (267) 514-7145 www.mugshotscoffeehouse.com

The Plough & the Stars

Category:	Has Vegan Items
Price Range:	$$
Comments:	In 2015, this Irish bar/restaurant vaulted into vegan prominence through the efforts of Chef Lenka Zivkovic, who had gone vegan six months earlier. The special vegan tasting-menu nights she created introduced many Philly vegans to a bold new voice, and she began showcasing her food at vegan events (she represented The Plough in the 2016 Vegan Mac and Cheese Mac-Down). An

accident injured her hand and forced her out of work for months, but as you're reading this now, she should be back overseeing vegan alternative dishes, vegan specials, and events. This place is definitely worth checking out.

Contact: 123 Chestnut St. (door is actually on 2nd St.)
(215) 733-0300
www.ploughstars.com

Qt

Category:	Has Vegan Items
Price Range:	$
Favorite Eats:	TOFU BANH MI SANDWICH—Browned tofu strips, pickled carrots, cilantro, and cucumber (jalapeño optional)
	RICE PLATTER—Tofu with mushrooms and onions
	TOFU SUMMER ROLLS—Vegan version of Qt spring rolls (no shrimp)
Comments:	For a small Vietnamese restaurant with a small menu, this is a relatively vegan-friendly establishment, though currently there's no vegan mayo option for the Banh Mi, so it must be ordered without mayo. It is located just at the south end of Chinatown.
Contact:	48 N. 10th St.
	(267) 639-4520
	www.qtvietnamesesandwich.com/home.html

Revolution Taco

Category:	Has Vegan Items
Price Range:	$
Favorite Eats:	SMOKED MUSHROOM VEGAN TACO—Served with cabbage and avocado chimichurri sauce FRIED CURRIED CAULIFLOWER—Served with guacamole, potato sticks, sesame seeds, and cilantro CHICKPEA VEGGIE BURGER—Can also be enjoyed as a burrito
Comments:	While the menu of this 2016-minted taco joint off of Rittenhouse Square is still pretty heavily meat-oriented, it has enough for vegans to choose from and to leave satisfied.
Contact:	2015 Walnut St. (267) 639-5681 www.therevolutiontaco.com

Slice

Category:	Very Vegan-Friendly
Price Range:	$
Favorite Eats:	PLAIN PIZZA—Cheese pizza using Daiya VEGGIE PIZZA—Topped with onions, mushrooms, peppers and/or olives, and Daiya "MEAT" PIZZA—Pepperoni and/or sausage pizza with vegan meat toppings from Vegan Commissary
Comments:	Both the regular and the whole-wheat crusts are vegan. Slice was one of the first restaurants in town to offer pizza with vegan cheese.

Contact: 1740 Sansom St.
(215) 557-9299
www.slicepa.com

Soy Cafe

Category:	Very Vegan-Friendly
Price Range:	$$

Favorite Eats: CHEESESTEAK WRAP—Grilled veg beef (seitan) topped with homemade vegan cashew cheese, fresh tomato, and spring mix (with optional grilled mushrooms) in wrap of your choice

TACO SALAD—Crunchy tortilla shell filled with spring mix, carrot, tomato, cucumber, avocado, jalapeño, grilled mushroom, and grilled soy chicken (seitan), served with homemade maple-mustard dressing

Comments: Soy Cafe is a mainstay of the Northern Liberties veg scene, and with its numerous vegan items, it may have helped pull several of the surrounding bars in a more vegan-friendly direction. Its baked gluten-free vegan donuts (a Zagat's Must-Try) are made from scratch with a whole-grain flour blend. They're dipped in dark chocolate and topped with dark chocolate chips, shredded coconut, toasted almond chips, or matcha cream. Seasonal flavors include blueberry pancake, strawberry cream, and peaches-and-cream.

Contact: 630 N. 2nd St.
(215) 922-1003
www.mysoycafe.com

Standard Tap

Category:	Has Vegan Items
Price Range:	$$
Favorite Eats:	EGGPLANT CAPONATA—Italian dish made with tomatoes, onions, peppers, and basil ROASTED SPAGHETTI SQUASH with Garlic BUTTERNUT SQUASH with Onions
Comments:	The "Woodman Jewel" oyster mushroom dish is also available in a vegan version (without cheese).
Contact:	901 N. 2nd St. (215) 238-0630 news.standardtap.com.s86406.gridserver.com

Strangelove's

Category:	Has Vegan Items
Price Range:	$$
Favorite Eats:	VEGAN NACHOS—Corn tortilla, refritos, soy chorizo, vegan cheese, and arugula RUSSIAN KALE—Beets, farro, soy beans, pecans, and creamy sumac dressing MUFFALETTA—Served with olive spread and garlic mayo on a ciabatta roll
Comments:	Starting with one or two options, Strangelove's has become even more vegan friendly within the past couple years. In fall of 2016, it hosted a Vegan Beer Dinner.
Contact:	216 S. 11th St. (215) 873-0404 www.strangelovesbeerbar.com

Su Xing House

Category:	Very Vegan-Friendly
Price Range:	$$
Favorite Eats:	GENERAL TSO SEITAN
	KUNG PAO DRIED TOFU WITH PEANUTS
	AS-YOU-WISH—Tofu skin filled with golden mushroom, black mushroom, dried tofu, and Chinese celery, served with water chestnut and asparagus
Comments:	Su Xing is mostly vegan with a few egg dishes that are marked as such on the menu. There are many inventive appetizers and sides as well as more standard "mock-meat" dishes.
Contact:	1508 Sansom St.
	(215) 564-1419
	www.suxinghouse.com

Sweetgreen

Category:	Very Vegan-Friendly
Price Range:	$$
Favorite Eats:	BUILD-YOUR-OWN BOWLS—Bases of greens and grains topped with choice of carrots, tomatoes, shredded cabbage, spicy sunflower seeds, raw beets, toasted almonds, red onion, hot chickpeas, basil, pears, raw pecans, spicy broccoli, roasted sweet potatoes, corn, apples, and tortilla chips
	SHROOMAMI—Wild rice, shredded kale, raw beets, bean sprouts, basil, spicy sunflower seeds, warm portobello mix, roasted sesame tofu, and miso sesame ginger dressing

SPICY SABZI—Baby spinach, shredded kale, roasted sesame tofu, spicy broccoli, raw beets, organic carrots, spicy quinoa, bean sprouts, basil, red chili, and carrot chili vinaigrette

Comments: "Premium" items include roasted curry cauliflower and herb falafel, and there are ten different vegan dressings. For such an earnest, "sustainable" approach, one might expect more than a couple on-menu vegan creations, but as is, there are still a lot of fresh, colorful foods vegans can easily find and enjoy at these spots.

Contact: 3925 Walnut St.
(215) 386-1365

924 Walnut St.
(215) 454-6770

1821 Chestnut St.
(215) 665-9710
www.sweetgreen.com

Tattooed Mom

Category: Very Vegan-Friendly

Price Range: $$

Favorite Eats: VEGAN BURGER—Served on a roll with poblano peppers and avocado cream (on special on Wednesdays from noon to midnight)
VEGAN PHILLY STEAK—Contest-contending version of Philly cheesesteak

Comments: A frequent spot for Philly Vegan Drinks, this South Street bar has a casual, funky charm that many others only aspire to. Part of the charm, of course, is its appeal to vegans. In addition to the dishes listed previously, the menu has many vegetarian items that can be veganized upon request. And the full veggie menu is half price every Meatless Monday from noon to 10 p.m. Going forward, Tattooed Mom said it is planning to expand the vegan sandwich menu.

Contact:	530 South St. (215) 238-9880 www.tattooedmomphilly.com

Veggie Lovers

Category:	Very Vegan-Friendly
Price Range:	$$
Favorite Eats:	PAN-FRIED TOFU in Scallion Ginger Sauce or in Toon Leaves Sauce ALMOND AND CASHEW VEG. CHICKEN SPIRAL SEAWEED in Rice Wine Sauce
Comments:	This Asian restaurant on the northwest end of Chinatown is very close to all-vegan but has a couple vegetarian options. It specializes in matching dishes with healthful Chinese teas.
Contact:	225 N. 11th St. (215) 226-6688 www.veggielovers.net

Zahav

Category:	Very Vegan-Friendly
Price Range:	$$
Favorite Eats:	CREMINI MUSHROOMS—Served with Israeli couscous, green tehina (i.e., tahini), and celery

SPICED EGGPLANT WITH HARISSA—Served with black lentils and garlic tehina

MASBACHA—Hummus served with warm chickpeas

Comments: Known in Philly for its perfectly pitched hummus and associated Middle Eastern dishes, Zahav pushes that envelope with additional fruit and mushroom dishes that are vegan off the menu or can be made so. It also includes large-platter pricing for parties of four or more.

Contact: 237 St. James Place
(215) 625-8800
www.zahavrestaurant.com

South Philly

Grindcore House Cafe

Category:	Vegan
Price Range:	$
Favorite Eats:	GREEN-WICH SANDWICH—Avocado, hummus, spinach, tomato, cucumber, and seed mix COCONUT-MILK LATTE—This and the other cappuccinos, lattes, and espressos are available with a variety of vegan creamers FRESH BAGEL—Served with house-made vegan chive cream cheese
Comments:	Grindcore House was the first institution in Philadelphia to put "vegan" on its main outdoor sign and hosted the first final judging event of the Best Vegan Cheesesteak in Philly Contest. In addition to the aforementioned items, it is also the city's largest-volume seller of baked goods from Dottie's Donuts, Vegan Treats, and Crust Bakery.
Contact:	1515 S. 4th St. (215) 839-3333 www.grindcorehouse.com

Miss Rachel's Pantry

Category:	Vegan
Price Range:	$$
Favorite Eats:	POTATO–CARAMELIZED ONION KNISHES—Little savory pastries filled with mashed Yukon golds and caramelized onions (A veganized Jewish delicacy.) GRILLED CHEESE—Homemade cheese on homemade challah bread CHOCOLATE CAKE—A triple layer, decadent chocolate cake, sold by the slice MATZO BALL SOUP—Somehow fluffy and dense at the same time, in a comforting broth
Comments:	A longtime vegan caterer in Philly, "Miss Rachel" Klein built up a clientele with regular weekday lunch deliveries and opened the current luncheonette in South Philly in 2014. It's open for brunch Tuesday through Sunday and for dinner on Friday and Saturday at one communal farmhouse table. Behind the quaint, homespun trappings is some of the best vegan food in Philadelphia, including amazing homemade vegan cheeses and cheese spreads.
Contact:	938 S. Chadwick St. (215) 798-0053 www.missrachelspantry.com

Vegan Commissary

Category:	Vegan
Price Range:	$$
Favorite Eats:	BREAKFAST HASH—Served with smoked tempeh and poached avocado

BRUNCH SANDWICH—Tofu-scramble patty with homemade scrapple and/or bacon
MEATBALL SUB—Served with tomato sauce, tofu ricotta, and spinach

Comments: The in-store market is open midday seven days a week and will be opening for breakfast starting in October (hopefully). There are also monthly Chef's Table brunches. The Commissary's products are found in DiBruno Bros. stores and in Mom's Organic Markets in Philly. The Brunch Sandwich is available at Good Karma coffee shops, and the Veggie Burger is available at P'unk Burger and "South and Porter."

Contact: 1429 Wolf St.
(215) 964-3232
www.vegancommissary.com

Vegan-Friendly

Adobe Cafe

Category: Very Vegan-Friendly

Price Range: $$

Favorite Eats: SEITAN TIPS SANDWICH—Served with vegan jalapeño mayo
SEITAN TACOS—Served with vegan sour cream
VEGGIE BURGER—Served with vegan cheese

Comments: Adobe was one of the first restaurants in Philadelphia to replicate most of its standard menu in a vegetarian, then vegan, version. It offers standard Tex-Mex fare with attention to detail, with some of your favorites veganized.

Contact: 919 E. Passyunk Ave.
(215) 551-2243
www.adobecafephilly.com

American Sardine Bar

Category: Very Vegan-Friendly

Price Range: $$

Favorite Eats: VEGGIE FLATBREAD—Served folded like a sandwich on house-made bread with dry-roasted portobellos, mixed zucchinis, alfalfa sprouts, crispy farro, and fried chickpeas, topped with homemade vegan ranch made with aquafaba
GRILLED BROCCOLI—Served with house-made hoisin sauce and sesame seeds
BEER-BATTERED ONION RINGS

Comments: American Sardine Bar also offers a meat-free, dairy-free cheesesteak using Blackbird seitan. Current sourcing of rolls indicates that they may not be vegan—best to ask when you're there if this option appeals.

Contact: 1800 Federal St.
(215) 334-2337
www.americansardinebar.com

Bitar's

Category: Has Vegan Items

Price Range: $$

Favorite Eats: GRILLED FALAFEL SANDWICH—Lettuce, tomato, parsley, and pickled turnips with sesame dressing

VEGETARIAN COMBO—Grilled falafel, grape leaves, babaghanoush, and pita

TABBOULEH SALAD—Cracked wheat, parsley, tomato, onion, lemon juice, and olive oil served on a bed of lettuce

Comments:	Bitar's is known as one of the top places to go for Middle Eastern and Mediterranean food in Philly. Many dishes are veganizable with the omission of feta and/or yogurt sauce.
Contact:	947 Federal St. (215) 755-1121 www.bitars.net

Cafe Valentino

Category:	Has Vegan Items
Price Range:	$$
Favorite Eats:	VEGAN SOUPS RISOTTO WITH MUSHROOMS VEGGIE PLATE—Plate of fresh vegetables
Comments:	This is an Italian restaurant that does not have a vegan menu but does have a vegan soup every day and sometimes does special vegan tasting events, such as the Spring Feast in early 2016 with Christina Pirello and Frank Olivieri Jr.
Contact:	1245 S. 3rd St. (215) 336-3033 www.caffevalentino.com

Cantina Los Caballitos

Category:	Very Vegan-Friendly
Price Range:	$$
Favorite Eats:	SEITAN ANTICUCHOS—Seitan skewers, smoked poblano crema, with a red quinoa and cucumber spicy peanut salad VEGAN BEEF BURRITO—Flour tortilla with rice, black beans, onions, and cilantro VEGAN FAJITAS—Served with house-smoked tofu and seitan
Comments:	One of Mark McKinney's signature vegan-enhanced bar menus, this South Philly sister to Northern Liberties' Cantina Dos Segundos also offers vegan nachos.
Contact:	1651 E. Passyunk Ave. (215) 755-3550 www.cantinaloscaballitos.com

Essene

Category:	Very Vegan-Friendly
Price Range:	$$
Favorite Eats:	BRAISED TOFU LENTIL PATTIES TOFU BROCCOLI SALAD
Comments:	Essene is a health-foods grocery with a hot bar. Items usually available from the hot bar include the previously listed items as well as sautéed bok choy, green beans with garlic (and sometimes with tofu), and roasted veggies such as cauliflower and potatoes. All soups and bakery items are vegan.

Contact:	719 S. 4th St.
	(215) 922-1146
	www.essenemarket.com

Honey's Sit 'N Eat

Category:	Has Vegan Items
Price Range:	$$
Favorite Eats:	TOFU SCRAMBLE—Served with turmeric, peppers, and garlicky cumin
	HOUSE-MADE VEGGIE BURGER—Vegan if ordered on vegan bread instead of brioche
	VEGAN ENFRIJOLADAS—Beans, tofu, and microgreen salad
Comments:	This diner-style venue emphasizes good ol' home-style American fare but puts an interesting spin on many items, with many veganizable dishes via the omission of the dairy component.
Contact:	2101 South St.
	(215) 732-5130
	www.honeyssitneat.com

The Pub on Passyunk East (P.O.P.E.)

Category:	Very Vegan-Friendly
Price Range:	$$
Favorite Eats:	CHEESESTEAK—Served with seitan and house-made cashew cheese
	SEITAN FINGERS—Served with BBQ-sauce french fries
	CRISPY GARBANZO BEANS—Tossed in paprika and lemon zest

Comments:	This bar, which frequently places in the top ten of the Best Vegan Cheesesteak in Philly Contest, also boasts vegan nachos and cheese fries using the house-made cashew cheese. It often has vegan tomato soup as well.
Contact:	1501 E. Passyunk Ave. (215) 755-5125 www.pubonpassyunkeast.com

P'unk Burger

Category:	Very Vegan-Friendly
Price Range:	$$
Favorite Eats:	"PULLED PORTOBELLO" SANDWICH—Served with tomatoes, onions, and P'unk vegan steak sauce, topped with sweet potato fries GRILLED PORTOBELLO SANDWICH
Comments:	P'unk Burger also has a veggie burger (from Vegan Commissary) and a roasted vegetable sandwich. In addition, it always has one or more vegan flavors of Little Baby's ice cream and specializes in vegan milkshakes using this and almond milk or soy milk.
Contact:	1823 E. Passyunk Ave. (215) 468-7865 www.punkburger.com

Royal Tavern

Category:	Very Vegan-Friendly
Price Range:	$$
Favorite Eats:	MUSHROOM AND SMOKY VEGAN BACON BURGER

SEITAN CHEESESTEAK (2015 contest winner)
VEGAN NACHOS

Comments: One of Mark McKinney's signature vegan-enhanced bar menus, Royal Tavern is a cozy South Philly spot that won the 2015 Best Vegan Cheesesteak in Philly Contest and was a top contender in 2016 as well.

Contact: 937 E. Passyunk Ave.
(215) 389-6694
www.royaltavern.com

Slice

Category: Very Vegan-Friendly

Price Range: $

Favorite Eats: PLAIN PIZZA—Cheese pizza using Daiya
VEGGIE PIZZA—Topped with onions, mushrooms, peppers and/or olives, and Daiya
"MEAT" PIZZA—Pepperoni and/or sausage pizza with vegan meat toppings from Vegan Commissary

Comments: Both the regular and the whole-wheat crusts are vegan. Slice was one of the first restaurants in town to offer pizza with vegan cheese.

Contact: 1180 S. 10th St.
(215) 463-0868
www.slicepa.com

South Philadelphia Taproom

Category: Very Vegan-Friendly

Price Range: $$

Favorite Eats:	FRIED TOMATO PO' BOY—Served with spicy vegan ranch, lettuce, and red onion
	GRILLED EGGPLANT—Served with polenta and tapenade
	ROASTED GREEN MEADOW CARROTS—Served in tahini, sumac, and preserved lemon
Comments:	This is a gastropub with a good number of interesting choices. The "Favorite Eats" items are from the dinner menu. The brunch menu includes Vegetable Tofu Scramble, Homefries with Homemade Ketchup, and Breakfast Tacos (green beans, guacamole, and refried beans) that are vegan if ordered without eggs.
Contact:	1509 Mifflin St.
	(215) 271-7787
	www.southphiladelphiataproom.com

The Tasty

Category:	Very Vegan-Friendly
Price Range:	$$
Favorite Eats:	THE HOT MESS—Dirty Jersey sandwich (faux pork roll/egg/cheese) with jalapeños on a Philly Bread Everything Muffin
	THE SPINACH AND SOYSAGE SCRAMBLE—Tofu scramble with soysage, spinach, caramelized onions, and Teese mozzarella
	FRIED CHIK'N SAMMY—Fried chik'n, spicy mayo, coconut bacon, lettuce, and tomato on a Kaiser roll
Comments:	Launching in 2016, this veggie diner stumbled a little out of the gate by calling itself "vegan" while offering cow's-milk creamer for its specially

curated coffees. However, the noncoffee menu is vegan. On the whole, The Tasty is stocked with varied and appealing options, including a much-buzzed-about vegan breakfast lineup.

Contact: 1401 S. 12th St.
(267) 457-5670
https://www.twitter.com/thetastyphilly

Triangle Tavern

Category: Very Vegan-Friendly

Price Range: $$

Favorite Eats: "ROAST BEEF" SANDWICH—Blackbird seitan sliced thin with roulade, caramelized onions, and optional horseradish vegan mayo
SEITAN CHEESESTEAK (2016 contest finalist)—Blackbird seitan with mushrooms, onions, and peppers on long roll
VEGAN MEATBALL SANDWICH—Served with broccoli rabe

Comments: One of Mark McKinney's signature vegan-enhanced bar menus, Triangle Tavern is a reboot of a cherished South Philly bar founded in 1933. Unlike its original incarnation, the reboot includes many vegan specialties, such as vegan nachos and buffalo seitan "wings." Another standout is the vegan scrapple, which McKinney, in a 2016 article, said was "outselling the original" animal-based version.

Contact: 1338 S. 10th St.
(215) 800-1992
www.triangletavernphilly.com

The Wild Burrito

Category:	Very Vegan-Friendly
Price Range:	$
Favorite Eats:	VEGAN BUFFALO BURRITO—Vegan cheese, Buffalo seitan, sauce, black beans, and vegan ranch dressing
	VEGAN AL PASTOR BURRITO—Achiote-marinated seitan, grilled pineapple, black beans, cilantro lime rice, pickled red onions, and vegan ranch dressing
	VEGAN NACHOS
Comments:	A simple Tex-Mex joint where most items have a vegan alternative version. As this book went to press, Wild Burrito added Cauliflower "Wings" to the menu, made with coconut milk and breaded with crumbled tortilla chips.
Contact:	2015 E. Moyamensing Ave.
	(215) 336-9453
	www.thewildburritophiladelphia.com

Northeast/Northwest

Vegan

Happy Hippy

Category:	Vegan
Price Range:	$$
Favorite Eats:	PROTEIN ENCHILADA—Chickpeas, beans, peppers, and hemp hearts COCONUT QUINOA CURRY SOUTHWEST SALAD—Spring mix, sweet potatoes, quinoa, and spicy southwest dressing
Comments:	Happy Hippy's main hangout during the school year is at the Student Activities Center at Temple University (13th and Montgomery); there are usually also stands at Drexel (Urban Eatery) and University of the Sciences (Tasty Drakes). Happy Hippy also has a stand in the newly opened Whole Foods on Pennsylvania Avenue, featuring the Beet Burger and Southwest Salad.
Contact:	1755 N. 13th St. (484) 443-3166 www.happyhippyveg.com

The Juice Merchant

Category:	Vegan
Price Range:	$$
Favorite Eats:	PORTOBELLO BACON SANDWICH—Plus avocado, lettuce, and tomato for the "BLTA"
	ASIAN NOODLE SALAD—Rice noodles, carrots, broccoli, red cabbage, red onion, red pepper, scallions, and sesame ginger dressing
	COFFEELICIOUS SMOOTHIE—Coffee powder, banana, almond milk, and vanilla
Comments:	Located on Main Street in Manayunk, The Juice Merchant is an ideal lunch spot with light fare, many juices, green smoothies and fruit smoothies, inventive salads, banana whips, and assorted treats—all of them vegan. It is also a good place to find shots of wheatgrass.
Contact:	4330 Main St.
	(215) 483-8888
	www.thejuicemerchant.com

The Nile

Category:	Vegan
Price Range:	$
Favorite Eats:	CHICKEN 'N GRAVY
	COLLARD GREENS
	BBQ WHEAT MEAT
Comments:	The Nile, a longtime Germantown Avenue institution, encourages healthful eating among its customers both by offering health classes and by delivering tuned-up (lower sodium), animal-free versions of familiar dishes. In addition to

sandwiches, wraps, and mock-meat platters, they also offer fruit smoothies, salads, corn bread and sweet breads, vegan cheesecake, and vegan ice cream.

Contact: 6008 Germantown Ave.
(215) 843-6453
https://www.facebook.com/NileCafePhilly

Vegan-Friendly

Adobe Cafe—Roxborough

Category: Very Vegan-Friendly

Price Range: $$

Favorite Eats: SEITAN TIPS SANDWICH—Served with vegan jalapeño mayo
SEITAN TACOS—Served with vegan sour cream
VEGGIE BURGER—Served with vegan cheese

Comments: Adobe was one of the first restaurants in Philadelphia to replicate most of its standard menu in a vegetarian, then vegan, version. It offers standard Tex-Mex fare with attention to detail, with some of your favorites veganized.

Contact: 4550 Mitchell St.
(215) 483-3947
www.adobecafephilly.com

Couch Tomato Cafe

Category: Has Vegan Items

Price Range: $$

Favorite Eats: VEGAN PIZZA—Topped with Kite Hill cheese
and veggies
VEGAN "MEAT" PIZZA—Topped with Kite Hill
cheese and chopped seitan
BASIL-TOMATO BISQUE—Vegan version of a
longtime house favorite

Comments: Just off of Main Street in Manayunk, Couch
Tomato has offered Daiya-based vegan pizza for
many years and has recently switched to Kite Hill.
Their crust is vegan. Couch Tomato says, "We are
working on many more vegan options because we
do see the need."

Contact: 100–102 Rector St.
(215) 483-2233
www.thecouchtomato.com

Front Street Cafe

Category: Very Vegan-Friendly

Price Range: $$

Favorite Eats: BUFFALO CAULIFLOWER—Served with cucumber-
dill dressing
"SPAGHETTI AND MEATBALLS"—Spaghetti squash with
lentil meatballs and marcona (almond) parmesan
FISHTOWN QUESO—Smoked black beans, cashew
cheese whiz, avocado, chipotle salsa, and corn
tortilla chips

Comments: In addition to its signature Buffalo Cauliflower,
this cafe in the Frankford section of Philly (right
next to the "El") also has vegan breakfast items
such as quinoa oat porridge, vegetable hash with
tofu scramble, and acai bowls made with acai

banana whip, coconut, fresh seasonal fruits, and nuts-and-seeds granola.

Contact: 1253 N. Front St.
(215) 515-3073
www.frontstreetcafe.net

Honeygrow

Category: Very Vegan-Friendly

Price Range: $$

Favorite Eats: ROASTED TOMATO MISO KALE SALAD—Roasted tomato miso dressing, green kale, organic roasted spicy tofu, apples, carrots, roasted beets, red onions, radishes, and sesame sticks
RED COCONUT CURRY STIR-FRY—Red coconut curry sauce, rice noodles, organic roasted spicy tofu, pineapples, jalapeños, bean sprouts, scallions, and cilantro
CREATE YOUR OWN STIR-FRY WITH SESAME GARLIC SAUCE—Organic roasted spicy tofu, choice of vegetables and garnish, and choice of brown rice, rice noodles, Boston lettuce cups, or our freshly made whole-wheat noodles

Comments: Honeygrow is based on a stir-fry or noodle-bowl model, so there are plenty of components to include or leave out to create your favorite food.

Contact: 1601 N. Broad St. (Temple University)
(215) 279-7823
www.honeygrow.com

Little Baby's Ice Cream

Category:	Has Vegan Items
Price Range:	$$
Favorite Flavors:	Vanilla Coconut Cream
	Speculoos
	Chocolate Salt Malt
	Lychee Lemonade
Comments:	Flavors rotate, but usually around 40 percent of the menu is entirely nondairy. In addition to the two storefront locations, Little Baby's is often seen in scaled-down food-truck format at events and usually has at least one vegan flavor for those.
Contact:	2311 Frankford Ave.
	(267) 687-8567
	www.littlebabysicecream.com

Memphis Taproom

Category:	Very Vegan-Friendly
Price Range:	$$
Favorite Eats:	Smoked Coconut Club Sandwich—Smoked coconut "bacon" with tofu and tomato-based mayo
	Vegan Burger—Made with quinoa and white beans
	Spaghetti Sandwich—Served with homemade vegan meatballs
Comments:	This is another of Philly's bars working to provide interesting vegan options, in this case without relying on seitan and other "faux meat" dishes. The Taproom also has a mushroom grinder that can be ordered in a vegan version.

Contact: 2331 E. Cumberland St.
            (215) 425-4460
            http://memphistaproom.com

Pizza Brain

Category:	Has Vegan Items
Price Range:	$
Favorite Eats:	CHEESE PIZZA—Regular cheese pizza with Daiya VEGGIE PIZZA—Daiya cheese with onions, red peppers, mushrooms, caramelized onions, and Brussels sprouts DESSERT—Little Baby's ice cream
Comments:	Pizza Brain garnered as much attention for its decor (a quasi "Pizza Museum") as for its food. But with vegan cheese and Little Baby's vegan ice creams housed on the premises, it's a great vegan lunch spot.
Contact:	2313 Frankford Ave. (215) 291-2965 www.pizzabrain.org

Slice

Category:	Very Vegan-Friendly
Price Range:	$
Favorite Eats:	PLAIN PIZZA—Cheese pizza using Daiya VEGGIE PIZZA—Topped with onions, mushrooms, peppers and/or olives, and Daiya "MEAT" PIZZA—Pepperoni and/or sausage pizza with vegan meat toppings from Vegan Commissary

Comments:	Both the regular and the whole-wheat crusts are vegan. Slice also features vegan desserts from High Point Bakery. Additionally, this location in Fishtown (note that, despite the address, this is not near the intersection of 4th and Girard) is all-organic.
Contact:	431 E. Girard Ave. www.slicepa.com

Taj India Vegetarian Cuisine

Category:	Very Vegan-Friendly
Price Range:	$$
Favorite Eats:	MUSHROOM BHAJI WITH RICE—With onions, garlic, and spices in a creamy tomato gravy VEGETABLE KABAB WRAP—Mixed vegetables baked in a clay oven and wrapped in a thin bread with lettuce, onions, tomatoes, and dressing VEGI-LOVERS PLATTER—Lunch special of one vegetable samosa, mixed vegetable curry or chana masala, and naan or rice
Comments:	This restaurant is a welcome oasis of vegan options in the scattershot region (so far!) of Far Northeast Philly. Vegan items are clearly labeled on menu, which in addition to main curries/rice/breads sections also offers "Vegetarian Chinese," "Tandoor Specials," and "South Indian Dishes." It also has five kinds of soup, all of them vegan.
Contact:	10863 Bustleton Ave. (215) 677-4400 www.taj-india.com

Weavers Way

Category: Has Vegan Items

Comments: Weavers Way is a co-op natural foods store with two locations in the same general area of town. Both the Mount Airy and the Chestnut Hill location carry many vegan lines—Daiya, Silk, Tofurky, and so on—and also more local products like Moshe's sandwiches and hummus. The Chestnut Hill location, which served as the site of the final judging event in the 2015 Best Vegan Cheesesteak in Philly Contest, has a hot bar that usually features vegan options, including vegan proteins such as seitan and/or tofu—that is, not just the pasta or potatoes or grilled veggies that are standard hot-bar choices.

Contact: Mt. Airy: 610 Carpenter Ln.
(215) 843-2350

Chestnut Hill: 8424 Germantown Ave.
(215) 866-9150
www.weaversway.coop

West Philadelphia

Vegan

Dottie's Donuts

Category:	Vegan
Price Range:	$
Favorite Donuts:	CHOCOLATE PISTACHIO BLUEBERRY VANILLA ORANGE COCONUT
Comments:	Launched by former Blackbird Pizzeria employees, Dottie's started as a supplier of Grindcore House Cafe and other vegan and vegan-friendly establishments and then opened a storefront location in spring of 2016. Various creative flavors of vegan donuts rotate from day to day. The chocolate-coffee-cardamom is a longtime favorite. For best results, follow @DottiesDonuts on Twitter to see what's on offer.
Contact:	4529 Springfield Ave. https://twitter.com/dottiesdonuts

HipCityVeg

Category:	Vegan
Price Range:	$$
Favorite Eats:	CRISPY HIPCITY RANCH—Gardein patty with a peppercorn-ranch dressing, pickles, lettuce, tomato, and onion on whole-wheat roll
	PHILLYSTEAK—Pulled seitan steak, grilled onion, mushroom, lettuce, tomato, and organic ketchup on a whole-wheat long roll
	ZIGGY BURGER—Classic burger with organic smoked tempeh and special sauce
	GROOTHIE—Green smoothie with organic apples, organic leafy greens, bananas, and seasonal fruit
Comments:	This vegan fast-food spot opened in March 2012 and quickly became a favorite lunch spot for Rittenhouse Square–area workers and residents. Cory Booker specifically mentioned HipCity and its "line down the block" as an indicator of people's interest in eating "good vegan food." From day one, the most popular sandwich has been the Crispy HipCity Ranch, which includes battered chick'n, lettuce, tomato, onion, pickle, and peppercorn ranch. HipCity reminds you that "you can also choose to toss the chick'n patty in buffalo sauce to spice it up!" In addition to the healthful Groothie, HCV also offers chocolate vegan milkshakes and other seasonal shakes.
Contact:	214 S. 40th St.
	(267) 244-4342
	www.hipcityveg.com

Vegan-Friendly

Atiya Ola's Spirit First Foods

Category:	Very Vegan-Friendly
Price Range:	$$
Favorite Eats:	STIR-FRY—Served with vegan burger and/or spicy vegan sausage
	PARTY SLAW—Coleslaw with carrots, nuts, and pineapple
	BLACK BEAN WRAP—Served with peppers, onions, and Vegenaise
Comments:	A healthful cafe on the outskirts of University City.
Contact:	4505 Baltimore Ave.
	(215) 939-3298
	www.universitycity.org/restaurants/atiya-olas -spirit-first-foods

Beefsteak

Category:	Very Vegan-Friendly
Price Range:	$$
Favorite Eats:	FRIDA KALE VEGGIE BOWL
	KIMCHI-WA VEGGIE BOWL
	GAZPACHO BOWL
Comments:	Located in the main student union for the University of Pennsylvania, Beefsteak draws the curious, veg-curious, and veg-centered from all over with a simple menu based on build-your-own bowls and salad. The menu's proteins

	section is distinguished from most by its marking options that are *not* vegan.
Contact:	Houston Hall, 3417 Spruce St. (215) 898-5552 https://cms.business-services.upenn.edu/ dining/hours-locations-a-menus/retail-dining/ beefsteak.html

Clarkville

Category:	Very Vegan-Friendly
Price Range:	$$
Favorite Eats:	WARM CAULIFLOWER SALAD—Kale, radish, focaccia, pickled onion, and black pepper vinaigrette DANGER PIE—Garlic tomato sauce, shredded Daiya, oregano, and sea salt VEGGIE BANDIT—Fried cauliflower, pickled beet, kale, white bean puree, and lemon tahini, served in a homemade bread pocket
Comments:	In addition to the aforementioned menu items, Clarkville has several veggie options that can be made vegan by substituting vegan cheese.
Contact:	4301 Baltimore Ave. (215) 387-4992

Dock Street

Category:	Very Vegan-Friendly
Price Range:	$$
Favorite Eats:	WHITE BEAN PIZZA—White bean puree, crushed tomato, and portobello, topped with spinach salad

VEGAN PESTO WRAP—Artichokes, mushrooms, spinach, peppers, red onion, tofu, and sun-dried tomatoes wrapped in house-made pizza bread
HOUSE-MADE VEGAN BURGER—Roasted veggies, beets, and a little curry

Comments: In addition to inventive mains, this bar boasts fun starters like Trio Fries (white potatoes, sweet potatoes, and leeks), Fried Brussels Sprouts, and House-Made Hummus with walnuts, roasted peppers, olives, and grilled flatbread. Dock Street makes all its beers on-site, and a spokesperson stated that 99 percent of their beers are vegan.

Contact: 701 S. 50th St.
(215) 726-2337 (BEER)
www.dockstreetbeer.com

Fu Wah

Category:	Has Vegan Items
Price Range:	$
Favorite Eats:	TOFU BANH MI—Served on long roll with cilantro, carrots, and vegan mayo
Comments:	This minimarket stocks many packaged vegan foods that are hard to find outside of major chain supermarkets and also has a vegan cheesesteak.
Contact:	810 S. 47th St.
(215) 729-2993
www.fuwahminimarket.com

Hibiscus Cafe

Category:	Very Vegan-Friendly
Price Range:	$$
Favorite Eats:	SEITAN FAJITA—Served with stew beans and grilled veggies JAMAICAN JERK TOFU—Served with brown rice and greens SEITAN FAJITA—Served with stew beans and grilled veggies
Comments:	An expanded juice bar, Hibiscus offers plenty of the green stuff as well as a few well-chosen sandwiches, salads, and wraps. There is also a Vegetable Personal Pizza that consists of whole-wheat crust, veggies (peppers, onions, and kale), and vegan rice-based mozzarella (must specify). The fajita is also available in quesadilla form. The Hibiscus vegan cheesesteak was a finalist in the 2014 inaugural contest.
Contact:	4907 Catharine St. (215) 307-3749

Honeygrow

Category:	Very Vegan-Friendly
Price Range:	$$
Favorite Eats:	ROASTED TOMATO MISO KALE SALAD—Roasted tomato miso dressing, green kale, organic roasted spicy tofu, apples, carrots, roasted beets, red onions, radishes, and sesame sticks RED COCONUT CURRY STIR-FRY—Red coconut curry sauce, rice noodles, organic roasted

spicy tofu, pineapples, jalapeños, bean sprouts, scallions, and cilantro

CREATE YOUR OWN STIR-FRY WITH SESAME GARLIC SAUCE—Organic roasted spicy tofu, choice of vegetables and garnish, and choice of brown rice, rice noodles, Boston lettuce cups, or our freshly made whole-wheat noodles

Comments:	Honeygrow is based on a stir-fry or noodle-bowl model, so there are plenty of components to include or leave out to create your favorite food.
Contact:	3731 Walnut St. (University of Pennsylvania) (215) 222-0400 www.honeygrow.com www.clarkvillephilly.com

Little Baby's Ice Cream

Category:	Has Vegan Items
Price Range:	$$
Favorite Flavors:	VANILLA COCONUT CREAM SPECULOOS CHOCOLATE SALT MALT LYCHEE LEMONADE
Comments:	Flavors rotate, but usually around 40 percent of the menu is entirely nondairy. In addition to the two storefront locations, Little Baby's is often seen in scaled-down food-truck format at events and usually has at least one vegan flavor for those.
Contact:	4903 Catharine St. (215) 921-2100 www.littlebabysicecream.com

Local 44

Category:	Very Vegan-Friendly
Price Range:	$$
Favorite Eats:	SPICY SEITAN NUGGETS—Served with maple Dijon or hot sauce FRIED BRUSSELS SPROUTS—Served with soy-chili vinaigrette PASTRAMI SANDWICH—Spiced Seitan Reuben, Thousand Island, and house-made sauerkraut on rye
Comments:	This is a local beer joint with a surprising number of vegan-friendly options. It's a good place to watch the Phillies lose.
Contact:	4333 Spruce St. (215) 222-2337 www.local44beerbar.com

Mad Mex

Category:	Very Vegan-Friendly
Price Range:	$$
Favorite Eats:	FRIED MARINATED TOFU TACOS—Served with bean sprouts "ANGRY HIPPIE" BURRITO—Rice, beans, tofu sour cream, and Daiya cheese MARINATED TOFU WRAP—Served with vegan cheese and buffalo sauce
Comments:	This restaurant is a wacky Tex-Mex chain with a vegan-friendly emphasis. Mark Mebus of Blackbird Pizzeria told the Vegan City Philadelphia group that "Mad Mex deserves respect. They had vegan options labeled as such as far back as '99!"

Contact: 3401 Walnut St.
(215) 382-2221
www.madmex.com

Pizza.Wings.Steaks (PWS)

Category: Has Vegan Items

Price Range: $

Favorite Eats: VEGAN WINGS—House-made seitan battered, fried, and served with vegan hot sauce
VEGAN CHEESE STEAK—Seitan with Teese vegan cheese
HAND-CUT FRIES

Comments: At this establishment, there is not a large vegan menu for sure, but it's not that large a menu anyway. "P-Dubbz" is included more for its track record as a standard-issue neighborhood joint that also makes sure vegans get fed. The cheesesteak rolls may be vegan; as of early 2016, P-Dubbz could not confirm. Might want to ask or go for the wings!

Contact: 3235 Powelton Ave.
(215) 222-1397
www.pdubbz.com

White Dog Cafe

Category: Very Vegan-Friendly

Price Range: $$$

Favorite Eats: KENNETT SQUARE MUSHROOMS
YUKON POTATO HOME FRIES
HUMMUS TRIO

Comments: This cafe is one of the earliest food venues in
Philly (this is the original location) to emphasize
sustainability as an overriding principle for
its cuisine, although it continues to be more
vegetarian- than vegan-friendly. Sample items
listed previously are mainstay sides from the
regular menu, but there are always vegan items
on offer. Vegan selections rotate every three
weeks, while the rest of the menu changes over
according to the season.

Contact: 3420 Sansom St.
(215) 386-9224
www.whitedog.com

Suburbs

Vegan

Arnold's Way

Category:	Vegan
Price Range:	$$
Favorite Eats:	RAW VEGAN CHEESEBURGER RAW "TUNA" NORI WRAP—Served with collards CHOCOLATE MOUSSE PIE
Comments:	A little far afield in Lansdale, Arnold's Way is one of the "Olde Original" vegan venues from Philly, having established a raw-foods presence on Main Street in Manayunk in 1992, flourishing there for many years before decamping for the 'burbs. It is also known for banana whips and smoothies.
Contact:	319 W. Main St., #4, Lansdale, PA (215) 361-0116 www.arnoldsway.com

Flora

Category:	Vegan
Price Range:	$$$
Favorite Eats:	BEET TARTARE—Beets, red onion, capers, pickled mustard seeds, lemon, and toast points BLACK-EYED PEA FRITTERS—Served with spicy tomato and eggplant relish LENTIL AND BLACK BEAN CHILI—Served with vegan sour cream and scallion
Comments:	A supercozy fine-dining restaurant just North of Philly, Flora follows a quasi–prix fixe model in that there are a set number of courses for a standard price. In each course, there are three or four things to choose from. Instead of black bean chili, one might choose Roasted and Stuffed Squash, which comes with mushroom, kale, red pepper, and barley with mushroom gravy. One recent dessert course example is the Spiced Cake, served with roasted persimmons and glazed walnuts. Flora's menu changes entirely from season to season according to what's locally available in the freshest form.
Contact:	307 York Rd., Jenkintown, PA (215) 779-7945 www.florajenkintown.com

Gangster Vegan Organics—Norristown

Category:	Vegan
Price Range:	$$
Favorite Eats:	SPICED FALAFEL WRAP—Sunflower seeds, carrot, garlic, cumin, cayenne, cilantro, parsley,

date-ginger spread, and pink salt, in a collard
green wrap
RAPPERS DELIGHT SMOOTHIE—Pineapple, date,
orange, apple, and maca powder, HPS
KALE CHIPS—Plain or cheesy garlic variety

Comments: This raw organic juice bar has a full range of
juices, tonics, elixirs, and smoothies, as well
as lunch-ready sandwiches, noodle bowls, and
desserts.

Contact: 2454 W. Main St., Norristown, PA
(610) 630-1600
www.gangstervegan.com

Gangster Vegan Organics—Phoenixville

Contact: 6 Gay St., Phoenixville, PA
(610) 616-0000
See details above

Luhv Bistro

Category: Vegan

Price Range: $

Favorite Eats: BLACK BEAN PLANTAIN ROASTED POBLANO
BURGERS—Gluten-free bun available
SWEET POTATO JALAPEÑO SOUP
CAESAR SALAD—Kale, romaine, chickpea croutons,
and vegan Caesar dressing

Comments: Luhv is a company that has been making black
bean burgers since 2015 and selling to vegan-
friendly outlets mainly in the Philly suburbs. In
late October 2016, the operation opened a bistro

on a corner in downtown Hatboro, which is just
northwest of Far Northeast Philadelphia.

Contact: 101 N. York Rd., Hatboro, PA
(903) 600-5848 (LUHV)
www.LUHVFOOD.com

Raw Can Roll Cafe

Category:	Vegan
Price Range:	$$
Favorite Eats:	BLT—Smoked tempeh bacon, lettuce, tomato, and homemade mayo PAD THAI—Zucchini noodles, bean sprouts, veggies, and peanut ginger sauce MINT CHOCOLATE SMOOTHIE—Almond milk, banana, vanilla, mint, cacao, and agave
Comments:	Raw Can Roll offers a varied menu of standard items done as raw cuisine, along with many juices, smoothies, and hearty salads.
Contact:	767 W. Lancaster Ave., Wayne, PA (484) 580-8454 http://rawcanrollcafe.eat24hour.com

Sprig and Vine

Category:	Vegan
Price Range:	$$
Favorite Eats:	SEARED SCALLION-JASMINE RICE CAKES—Served with lemongrass ponzu stir-fry, grilled asparagus, sesame-ginger sauce, and basil-radish slaw

TEMPEH—Miso, maple and mustard-glazed, with potato mash, braised greens, and horseradish-cashew cream

FORBIDDEN BREAKFAST BURRITO—Scrambled tofu, forbidden black rice, avocado, pickled carrot, and sesame-kimchi aioli on whole-wheat tortilla

TIRAMISU—White chocolate cream, coffee-soaked olive oil cake, bourbon-chocolate sauce, and coconut–coffee bean ice cream

Comments: Located in New Hope, Sprig and Vine is as close as you can get these days to Horizons Cafe, as it is run by Horizons sous-chef Ross Olchvary. It's classy without being pretentious, delicious without overthinking anything. In addition to the aforementioned offerings, Sprig and Vine usually features appetizers such as Edamame Falafel with lemon kosho tahini, Green Onion Pancake with maitake mushroom and sesame-tomato jam, and Za'atar-Grilled Oyster Mushrooms with seared potato pavé and saffron aioli.

Contact: 450 Union Square Dr., New Hope, PA
(215) 693-1427
www.sprigandvine.com

Su Tao Cafe

Category:	Vegan
Price Range:	$
Favorite Eats:	FOREVER YOUNG—Sautéed string beans and veggie turkey served in a scallion pancake
	PAN-FRIED CRISPY NOODLES WITH VEGGIE SEAFOOD

HAPPY FAMILY—Three kinds of veggie seafood, veggie chicken, and beef with vegetables in white sauce

Comments: A longtime vegan fixture on the western end of the Main Line, Su Tao is a bit of a hike from Center City Philadelphia but has an abundance and variety of creative vegan offerings that make it worth the trip. The venue has also often served as a meeting place for Philly's suburban vegan community.

Contact: Great Valley Shopping Center, 81 Lancaster Ave., Malvern, PA
(610) 651-8886
www.sutaocafe.com

Sweet Freedom Bakery—Bryn Mawr

Category:	Vegan
Price Range:	$$
Favorite Eats:	MAGIC BAR—Shortbread crust with chocolate glaze and coconut flakes SALTED CARAMEL CUPCAKES SAMOA COOKIES—Caramel and toasted coconut
Comments:	This bakery carved out the niche of allergen-free, gluten-free baked goods in 2010. In addition to over-the-counter cupcakes, donuts, and other treats, Sweet Freedom does custom orders of cakes and pies. Originally some items included honey, but a rep assured me that all items are now honey-free.
Contact:	1039 Lancaster Ave. (610) 527-7323 www.sweetfreedombakery.com

Sweet Freedom Bakery—Collingswood

Contact:	577 Haddon Ave., Collingswood, NJ
	(856) 869-7322
	See details above

Vegan-Friendly

Frankie's on Fairview

Category:	Very Vegan-Friendly
Price Range:	$$
Favorite Eats:	CHIK'N & WAFFLES—Served with a maple/ sriracha drizzle
	BREAKFAST "MCMUFFIN"—Made with tofu
	ROASTED SPICY POTATO TACOS—Peppers, onions, potatoes, grilled corn, tomato, black bean vinegar slaw, and avocado on whole-wheat flour tortillas
Comments:	This restaurant was a finalist in the 2016 Best Vegan Cheesesteak in Philly Contest. It also has seitan "wings." Although it's located a ways out to the southwest of Philly, if you're doing anything else on the west side of town, it's probably worth a little jaunt. The owner works hard to make vegans happy.
Contact:	604 Fairview Rd., Woodlyn, PA
	(610) 543-2300
	www.frankiesonfairview.com

Honeygrow—Bala Cynwyd

Category:	Very Vegan-Friendly
Price Range:	$$

Favorite Eats: ROASTED TOMATO MISO KALE SALAD—Roasted tomato miso dressing, green kale, organic roasted spicy tofu, apples, carrots, roasted beets, red onions, radishes, and sesame sticks
RED COCONUT CURRY STIR-FRY—Red coconut curry sauce, rice noodles, organic roasted spicy tofu, pineapples, jalapeños, bean sprouts, scallions, and cilantro
CREATE YOUR OWN STIR-FRY WITH SESAME GARLIC SAUCE—Organic roasted spicy tofu, choice of vegetables and garnish, and choice of brown rice, rice noodles, Boston lettuce cups, or our freshly made whole-wheat noodles

Comments: Honeygrow is based on a stir-fry or noodle-bowl model, so there are plenty of components to include or leave out to create your favorite food.

Contact: 169 E. City Ave., Bala Cynwyd, PA
(610) 667-2573
www.honeygrow.com

Honeygrow—Radnor

Category: Very Vegan-Friendly

Price Range: $$

Favorite Eats: ROASTED TOMATO MISO KALE SALAD—Roasted tomato miso dressing, green kale, organic roasted spicy tofu, apples, carrots, roasted beets, red onions, radishes, and sesame sticks
RED COCONUT CURRY STIR-FRY—Red coconut curry sauce, rice noodles, organic roasted spicy tofu, pineapples, jalapeños, bean sprouts, scallions, and cilantro

CREATE YOUR OWN STIR-FRY WITH SESAME GARLIC SAUCE—Organic roasted spicy tofu, choice of vegetables and garnish, and choice of brown rice, rice noodles, Boston lettuce cups or our freshly made whole-wheat noodles

Comments:	Honeygrow is based on a stir-fry or noodle-bowl model, so there are plenty of components to include or leave out to create your favorite food.
Contact:	230 N. Radnor Chester Rd., Radnor, PA (610) 688-8393 www.honeygrow.com

Honeygrow—Cherry Hill

Contact:	1588 Kings Highway North (Ellisburg Shopping Center), Cherry Hill, NJ (856) 520-8122 See details above

Mad Mex

Category:	Very Vegan-Friendly
Price Range:	$$
Favorite Eats:	FRIED MARINATED TOFU TACOS—Served with bean sprouts "ANGRY HIPPIE" BURRITO—Rice, beans, tofu sour cream, and Daiya cheese MARINATED TOFU WRAP—Served with vegan cheese and buffalo sauce
Comments:	This restaurant is a wacky Tex-Mex chain with a vegan-friendly emphasis. Mark Mebus of Blackbird Pizzeria told the Vegan City

Philadelphia group that "Mad Mex deserves respect. They had vegan options labeled as such as far back as '99!"

Contact: 50 E. Wynnewood Rd., Wynnewood, PA
(484) 417-6932
www.madmex.com

Mi Lah Vegetarian

Category:	Vegan
Price Range:	$$
Favorite Eats:	PAN SEARED RAVIOLIS—Cashew nut cream, truffle oil, roasted cauliflower, and pepper topped with almond slice
	INDONESIAN ROLLS—Carrots, seitan, mushrooms, and celery wrapped in crispy rice paper and served with basil-avocado sauce
	FRESH-BAKED SHIITAKE TRUFFLE OIL CAKE—Topped with Mexican chili stew
Comments:	Mi Lah long had a presence in the heart of Center City but decamped a few years back for the 'burbs—namely, Ambler, up Route 309. This version is nearly vegan except for a few nonvegan options but always has plenty of vegan soups, salads, sides, entrées, and desserts.
Contact:	40 W. Skippack Pike, Ambler, PA
	(215) 646-1808
	www.milahvegetarian.com

Norma's Eastern Mediterranean Cuisine

Category:	Very Vegan-Friendly
Price Range:	$$
Favorite Eats:	VEGAN TOFU SHAWARMA—Served with caramelized onions, tomatoes, and tahini in a pita
	VEGAN MOUSSAKA—Breaded eggplant, stuffed seitan (Blackbird's), carrots, chickpeas, tomatoes, and green peppers with rice pilaf, topped with almond béchamel
	FALAFEL SALAD—Lettuce, tomatoes, pickled turnips, parsley, and falafel in tahini
Comments:	Lots of à la carte options like hummus and grape leaves make this a particularly vegan-friendly Middle Eastern menu. Cherry Hill is a few towns in on the Jersey side but very easy to access from the Ben Franklin Bridge.
Contact:	145 Barclay Farms Shopping Center, Cherry Hill, NJ
	(856) 795-1373
	www.normasrestaurant.com

White Dog Cafe

Category:	Very Vegan-Friendly
Price Range:	$$$
Favorite Eats:	KENNETT SQUARE MUSHROOMS
	YUKON POTATO HOME FRIES
	HUMMUS TRIO
Comments:	This cafe has two suburban locations that are quite close to one another, in Wayne and Haverford on the Main Line. White Dog was one of the earliest food venues in Philly to

emphasize sustainability as an overriding principle for its cuisine, although it continues to be more vegetarian- than vegan-friendly. Sample items listed previously are mainstay sides from the regular menu, but there are always vegan items on offer. Vegan selections rotate every three weeks, while the rest of the menu changes over according to the season.

Contact: Wayne: 200 W. Lancaster Ave., Wayne, PA (610) 225-3700

Haverford: 379 Lancaster Ave., Haverford, PA (610) 896-4556

Non-Site-Specific

Vegan

Crust Vegan Bakery

Category:	Vegan
Price Range:	$$
Favorite Eats:	CAKES—Vanilla, chocolate, lemon, carrot, coconut, gluten-free vanilla, and gluten-free chocolate
	COOKIES—Chocolate chip, oatmeal raisin, sugar, peanut butter, lemon, and shortbread
	BARS—Brownies, blondies, coffee cake, and peanut butter blondie
Comments:	Crust vegan treats are available at several locations around Philadelphia including HipCityVeg, Gold Standard in West Philly, and Red Hook Tea & Coffee on Fabric Row. Crust also sampled cookies for the attendees at the third annual Best Vegan Cheesesteak in Philly Contest.
Contact:	(931) 698-7676
	info@crustveganbakery.com
	http://www.crustveganbakery.com

Vegan-Friendly

Jerry's Kitchen

Category:	Has Vegan Items
Price Range:	$$
Favorite Eats:	VEGAN CHEESESTEAK—Seitan, vegan cheese, peppers, and onions on long roll
	FALAFEL BOWL—Served with three-grain (lentils, quinoa, and couscous) salad
	BLACK BEAN-WA BURGER—Black beans and quinoa topped with shaved beet slaw
Comments:	Jerry's vegan cheesesteak was a finalist in the 2015 contest. The food truck locations are posted daily on social media (https://twitter.com/jerrysfoodtruck).
Contact:	3225 Arch St.
	(610) 400-1532
	www.jerrys-kitchen.com

Kung Fu Hoagies

Category:	Very Vegan-Friendly
Price Range:	$
Favorite Eats:	BÁNH UÓT—Chewy rice noodles served cold with fried tofu, vegan sausage, lettuce, sprouts, basil, cucumber, jalapeño, vegan fish sauce, fried onion, and peanuts
	SPICY RAMEN—Springy ramen noodles with veggie chicken, sprouts, cucumber, cilantro, spicy pickles, fried onion, and lime
	VEGAN JERKY

Comments: Customers here can experience wraps, sandwiches, and rice bowls, all with a generally Asian theme with some standout Vietnamese-influenced items. The cart's offerings are thoroughly vegetarian and almost all are vegan, but the owners still maintain a couple nonvegan items, apparently to keep the pressure off. The cart is usually found in West Philly locations such as Clark Park, but it is occasionally also seen around South Philly.

Contact: (267) 344-6259
www.kungfuhoagies.com

Love Chunk Cookies

Category:	Vegan
Price Range:	$$
Favorite Eats:	CHOCOLATE CHIP
	CHOCOLATE-DIPPED SALTED PISTACHIO
	CHOCOLATE-DIPPED PEANUT BUTTER

Comments: These vegan cookies are increasingly available throughout the Philly area, especially including Weavers Way in Chestnut Hill, Whole Foods on Pennsylvania Avenue, and often at Fair Foods in the Reading Terminal Market. They are also available in the suburbs at all Kimberton Whole Foods locations and the Swarthmore Co-op.

Contact: West Chester, PA
www.lovechunkcookies.com

Magic Carpet Food Truck

Category:	Very Vegan-Friendly
Price Range:	$
Favorite Eats:	BAKED TOFU—Baked marinated tofu, salad, and dressing
	SEITAN GRINDER—Seitan pepper steak with cheese, salad, and sauce
	TEMPEH SALAD—Soybean cake on tossed salad with dressing
Comments:	Magic Carpet has been slinging vegan-friendly veggie food since the late twentieth century. I recall a daily cart in Rittenhouse Square that I used to patronize as a vegetarian, often getting the Baked Tofu or Magic Meatball Sandwich. This truck is now usually found between 35th and 37th off of Spruce Street on the University of Pennsylvania campus.
Contact:	https://www.facebook.com/pages/Magic -Carpet-Foods/130251873665043

About the Author

VANCE LEHMKUHL is the vegan columnist for the *Philadelphia Daily News*, covering the city's plant-based food scene in his print column *V for Veg* and philly.com blog "V for Vegan." His most recent book is *V for Veg: The Best of Philly's Vegan Food Column*, also published by Sullivan Street Press.

CPSIA information can be obtained
at www.ICGtesting.com
Printed in the USA
LVOW10s0927150117

521003LV00001B/94/P